PRAISE FOR NEVER THE SAME AGAIN

This anthology not only captures the revealing and illuminating insights into the Liberian people through the cultural lenses of young Americans, but also the complex, historic interactions between Liberians and Americans. It is easy to relate to the experiences of these latter-day "missionaries" as they live among, render critical service to, and befriend Liberians over the years.
—**Dr. D. Elwood Dunn**, the Alfred Walter Negley professor of political science emeritus, Sewanee: The University of the South, a Liberian citizen and a former minister of state for presidential affairs in the Tolbert administration

The Peace Corps' experience brings out the storyteller in all of us. This collection of inspiring stories and poems by Friends of Liberia (FOL) members captures those moments and memories that make the Peace Corps truly life-transforming. May this anthology find its way into schools and communities across the nation so that more of us can awaken to the world that awaits our quest for adventure and sense of mission.
—**Glenn Blumhorst**, president and CEO of the National Peace Corps Association (NPCA), RPCV Guatemala (1988-91)

NEVER THE SAME AGAIN

LIFE, SERVICE, AND FRIENDSHIP IN LIBERIA

EDITED BY
SUSAN E. GREISEN
SUSAN CORBETT
KAREN E. LANGE

NEVER THE SAME AGAIN

LIFE, SERVICE, AND FRIENDSHIP IN LIBERIA

EDITED BY
SUSAN E. GREISEN
SUSAN CORBETT
KAREN E. LANGE

Sidekick Press
Bellingham, Washington

Publisher's Note: This anthology represents the writers' recollection of their past. These true stories and poems are faithfully composed based upon memory, photographs, diary entries, or other supporting documents. Some names, places, and other identifying details have been changed to protect the privacy of those represented. Conversations between individuals are meant to reflect the essence, meaning, and spirit of the events described. Each individual author is responsible for the content of his or her work.

Sidekick Press
2950 Newmarket Street
Suite 101-329
Bellingham, Washington 98226
www.sidekickpress.com

Never the Same Again: Life, Service, and Friendship in Liberia
ISBN 978-1-7369351-5-6
LCCN 2022901028

Cover Design: Andrea Gabriel
Cover Photograph: Owen Hartford, Village of Zorgowee, Liberia, 1968

CONTENTS

Part II Turbulent Times

Part III Rebuilding Hope (The Latter Years)

Reference Materials

DEDICATION

This Anthology is dedicated to all who have served and continue to serve Liberia and her people.

All proceeds from the sale of this anthology will be donated to Friends of Liberia (FOL), sponsoring education, social, health, economic, and humanitarian programs that serve Liberia.

FOREWORD

BY ELLEN JOHNSON SIRLEAF
PRESIDENT OF LIBERIA. 2006-2018
NOBEL PEACE PRIZE RECIPIENT 2011

Sixty years ago, a new, young, American president, John F. Kennedy, offered an exciting new program to the world. Young Americans would be sent to help other countries with their expressed needs. President William Tubman was one of the first heads of state to welcome the Peace Corps.

A fresh-faced group of idealists arrived to work in our classrooms and clinics, fields and building projects, and, most amazingly, live the way we did. They discovered our culture, our way of dressing, ate and danced with us, learned our ways and decided they liked them. Then they went back to America singing our praises and inspiring many more to do the same.

Several decades later, during Liberia's civil wars, when most foreigners left Liberia, a small group started by those former Peace Corps volunteers in the United States calling itself Friends of Liberia summoned everyone who loved Liberia to become her voice in the world. They hosted our interim presidents, advocated to Congress on our behalf, and even started an email news service to inform Americans and Liberians as to what was happening in Liberia. They held conflict resolution workshops and invited individuals who represented the warring factions to come and talk. Eventually, at the urging of Friends of Liberia, the State Department appointed a Peace Corps alumnus diplomat to be its special envoy.

Throughout the conflict, the "Friends" provided emergency assistance including providing a medical doctor at Catholic Hospital. When the war finally ended, Friends of Liberia sponsored development projects helping us retrain and rebuild. And, they immediately started advocating for the Peace Corps to return to Liberia.

One of my first actions as president of Liberia was to request the Peace Corps start sending us teachers again. During my presidency, I tried to attend the swearing-in ceremony of each new group of arriving Peace Corps volunteers. I wanted to thank them for coming, to welcome them, and I knew many of them would become lifelong friends of my country and would have our best interests at heart.

Now this book has come out to tell us in sixty-three individual stories what it was like for Americans over all those decades to discover our culture. Underlying themes in these memories are mutual respect, innocence, wonder, and nostalgia. The beautiful details in these accounts attest to the freshness of these memories decades later. They come from a time when living in Liberia was transforming these authors, making their memories indelible. The memories of these Americans will be unforgettable to Liberians whose lives and chances were transformed by a good teacher, a lifesaving doctor, a wonderful friend.

Some of the authors were not Peace Corps volunteers. They are also members of Friends of Liberia and continue to work in our best interests. Just by telling these stories, they are introducing Liberia to new people who will never see her the same way again.

As we await the next wave of idealists to reach our shores, let this book say to its readers: "Liberia is worth knowing."

Some 4,200 Peace Corps volunteers have served in Liberia. I thank you all for your service and your lifelong dedication to Liberia.

INTRODUCTION

ABOUT THIS BOOK

"Ask not what your country can do for you—ask what you can do for your country." President John F. Kennedy's inaugural statement inspired Americans to serve their country for the cause of peace by living and working in the developing world. His vision created the Peace Corps in 1961, and the first volunteers arrived in Liberia in 1962. Sixty years later, in 2022, we celebrate this anniversary with our anthology, *Never the Same Again: Life, Service, and Friendship in Liberia.*

Storytelling has a long tradition throughout Africa. Elders have used stories to share their wisdom and knowledge through the generations, passing along their history, traditions, and lessons. Our anthology continues this tradition through stories about relationships that illuminate a cross-cultural awareness we can learn from and share with others. We offer a window into everyday village life: work in the classroom or the clinic; living among the people; relationships formed and lost; and the trials and tribulations of civil unrest and epidemics.

ABOUT THE AUTHORS

Our authors belong to Friends of Liberia (FOL), a nonprofit organization. We are former Peace Corps volunteers, Liberians, missionaries, medical relief workers, and contractors. Our service to Liberia mattered. Our footsteps left footprints—a human connection that has endured through a lifetime of service. This connection continues through FOL's mission to support Liberia by funding educational, social, economic, and humanitarian programs. Visit FOL.org.

WHY NOW?

Now, more than ever, is the time to share our stories. Countries, communities, and even families are divided over varying beliefs and values, whether it be religion, race, politics, pandemics, or climate change. How can we better understand and accept one another within these divisions? Many of the personal accounts in this anthology describe a culture unfamiliar to those who have not lived in Liberia. Our book provides a glimpse into the Liberian way of life, showing firsthand how living among its people fosters understanding and acceptance. The many people of Liberia who have survived the hardships of poverty, high morbidity and mortality, civil wars, and Ebola have something vitally important to show us about determination, resilience, survival, and hope. The relationships we developed with the people of Liberia instilled valuable lessons . . . ones that changed us forever.

HOW TO USE THIS BOOK

This collection of stories and poems is rich with takeaways to inform and inspire you about the power of human connection. You will learn more about the vital importance of being a global citizen and how you can help through FOL. We also encourage you to use these stories as teaching tools in your schools, faith-based communities, nonprofit or government agencies, publications, and social media. In the appendix you will find resources that help place these stories into context. You will also find information on a Global Connection Program where former Peace Corps volunteers who served in Liberia are available to share their experiences with you and your audiences.

Sit back and join us on our vivid journey back in time to a place and its people, loved by so many—the fascinating country of Liberia.

Susan E. Greisen
FOL Anthology Chief Editor

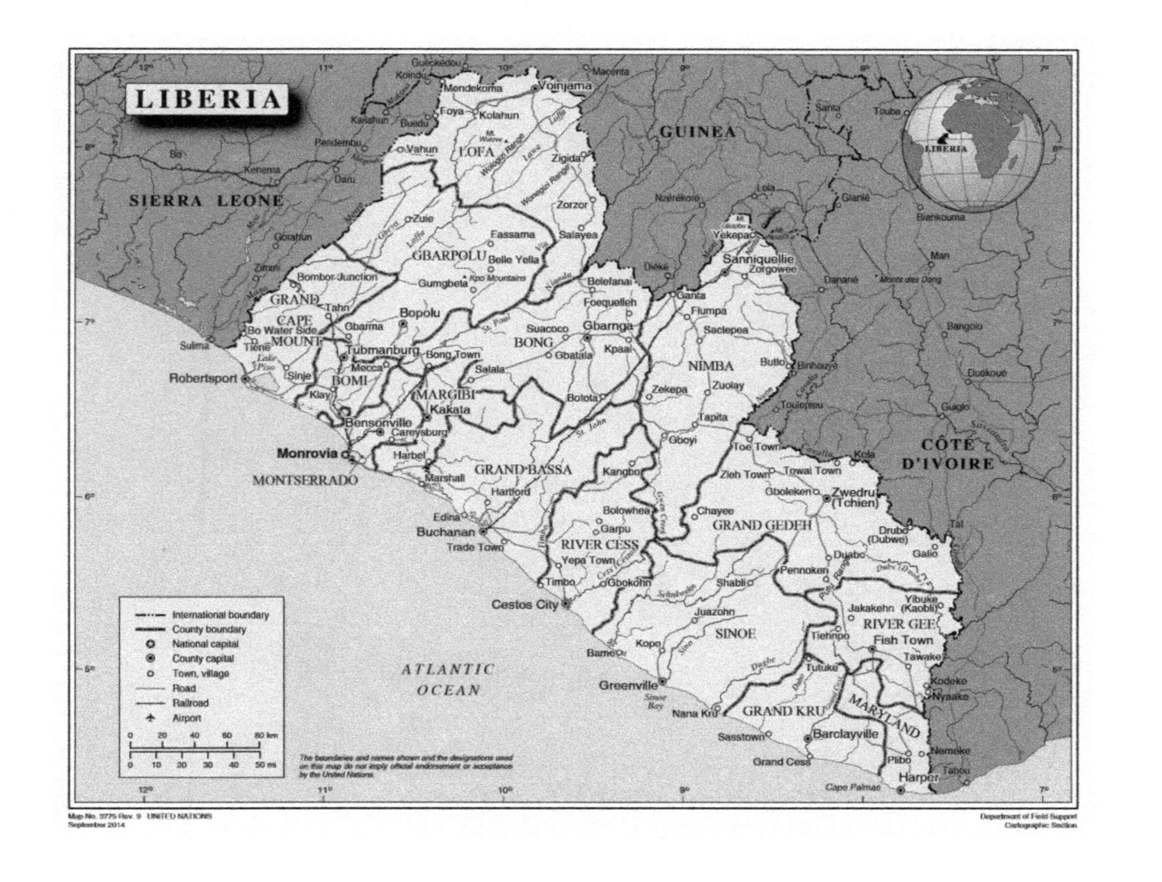

LIBERIA
SIERRA LEONE
GUINEA
CÔTE D'IVOIRE
ATLANTIC OCEAN
LOFA
GBARPOLU
GRAND CAPE MOUNT
BOMI
BONG
MARGIBI
MONTSERRADO
GRAND BASSA
NIMBA
RIVER CESS
GRAND GEDEH
SINOE
RIVER GEE
GRAND KRU
MARYLAND
Monrovia
Robertsport
Tubmanburg
Bopolu
Voinjama
Gbarnga
Kakata
Bensonville
Buchanan
Cestos City
Sanniquellie
Zwedru (Tchien)
Greenville
Fish Town
Barclayville
Harper
International boundary
County boundary
National capital
County capital
Town, village
Road
Railroad
Airport
The boundaries and names shown and the designations used on this map do not imply official endorsement or acceptance by the United Nations.
Map No. 3775 Rev. 9 UNITED NATIONS
September 2014
Department of Field Support
Cartographic Section

LIBERIA'S ABRIDGED TIMELINE

(1962–2020)

Freed slaves from the United States began settling the coast of West Africa in 1820 with the help of the American Colonization Society. After many died of disease, the settlers moved down the coast to the area that is now Monrovia, Liberia, in 1822. In 1847, they declared the independent nation of Liberia—Africa's first republic. Their motto: "The love of liberty brought us here." But the land they claimed through purchase and conquest had been inhabited for centuries by at least sixteen ethnic groups. Even after these indigenous people received the right to vote in 1946, they remained second-class citizens. A single party controlled by the Americo-Liberian minority ruled well into the twentieth century. When the Peace Corps volunteers arrived, President William V.S. Tubman, a descendant of settlers, had been in power for nearly two decades. Though the nation was stable and its economy growing, it was deeply divided, with a small elite holding most of the wealth and access to government positions.

1962

Peace Corps Volunteer Group 1 enters Liberia.

1971

President Tubman dies in office after ruling for twenty-seven years. His vice-president, William R. Tolbert, becomes president.

1975

Tolbert is reelected president amidst economic troubles, and calls for change.

1979

A government proposal to increase the price of rice, Liberia's staple food, in order to encourage local rice production and discourage rice imports, leads to riots in the capital of Monrovia.

1980

Master Sergeant Samuel K. Doe seizes power in a coup that leads to the killing of President Tolbert and becomes the first indigenous person to lead Liberia. Doe's People's Redemption Council executes thirteen of Tolbert's top officials. Many Americo-Liberians flee the country.

1985

Doe promises free and fair elections but rigs the result of the vote, declaring himself president. After a failed coup attempt by Thomas Quiwonkpa, Doe sends soldiers from his Krahn ethnic group to kill political opponents and members of the Mano and Gio ethnic groups, whom he sees as enemies.

1989

Charles Taylor, a former Doe official who fled the country after being accused of embezzlement, invades Liberia on Christmas Eve with a small group of rebels.

1990

Taylor's fighters, including child soldiers, overrun Doe's army. Peace Corps volunteers are evacuated in May. The rebels reach the capital by June. Both sides massacre members of ethnic groups they perceive as enemies. West African peacekeepers arrive, but rebels led by Prince Johnson, a breakaway commander, take much of the capital, capture Doe and torture and kill him. The peacekeepers take control of Monrovia to protect the interim government. Outside the capital, more rebel groups emerge, led by rival warlords from ethnic groups that support Doe.

1996

Faced with a stalemate, Taylor, the most powerful warlord, agrees to a cease-fire and elections.

1997

Charles Taylor is elected president in a vote observed by thirty-four members of Friends of Liberia.

1999

Anti-Taylor rebels invade from Guinea, starting Liberia's second civil war.

2003

Taylor flees to Nigeria as rebel factions from the north and south approach the capital.

2005

Ellen Johnson Sirleaf, a former Citibank executive and Director of the United Nations Development Program's Regional Bureau for Africa, who opposed Doe, is elected president, becoming Africa's first woman head of state.

2010

With Liberia stable and peaceful, the Peace Corps volunteers return.

2012

Taylor, extradited to The Hague, is found guilty of war crimes committed against civilians in neighboring Sierra Leone and sentenced to fifty years in prison.

2014

Ebola spreads across Liberia. The Peace Corps withdraws volunteers.

2016

Liberia is declared Ebola-free. The Peace Corps volunteers return.

2017

Former soccer star George Weah is elected president after Sirleaf's second term.

2019

A financial crisis causes the Peace Corps to evacuate some volunteers.

2020

With the spread of COVID-19, the Peace Corps evacuates the rest of Liberia's volunteers as the agency suspends operations worldwide.

PART I
BUILDING A FOUNDATION
(THE EARLY YEARS)

THE TOUGHEST JOB YOU'LL EVER LOVE

BY PHILLIP DESAUTELL

After graduating high school in 1965, I completed my Marine Corps active duty, began serving my active reserves duty, and got married. In the fall of 1969, I started night school at Texas Tech University. Rushing to my first class after work, I saw a sign with large block letters—"PEACE CORPS, IT'S THE TOUGHEST JOB YOU'LL EVER LOVE"—above a black-and-white photo of an African village scene with children playing in front of a grass roof hut.

I skidded to a stop at the temporary desk of a Peace Corps recruiter. He was packing up for the day, but he looked up and said, "May I help you?"

"No," I said, "I'm on my way to my first night school class after work."

"If you're in night school," he said, "what work do you do during the day?"

"I'm a machinist," I said.

He stopped packing the box of brochures. "Can you take a few minutes to talk?"

I was running late, but his interest prompted me to say "Yes." That one word changed the trajectory of my whole life.

The recruiter introduced himself and asked me to describe my work. When I finished, he said, "This is incredible! The Peace Corps recently began recruiting non-college graduate, technically skilled craftsmen. There's a program serving in a technical school in Malawi looking for a machinist to teach machine shop practices. Would you be interested in applying?"

My heart started beating like a trip hammer, and my head felt light. This was my best dream come true. Then, almost as suddenly, my heart sank. "Well, there's a problem," I said. "I'm married."

"That doesn't matter," he said. "Peace Corps has anticipated that a skilled craftsman might not be single. We'll find a program for your wife if you're accepted."

My hand trembled as I took the application forms from him. I had dreamed of being in the Peace Corps since its creation by my idol, President Kennedy. I had been drawn to living in Africa since eighth grade, devouring every National Geographic in my school's library. That had been the sole motivation for taking the SAT four years after high school and applying to Texas Tech while still working full-time. I imagined that, down the road, after getting a degree, my wife, Cheryl, and I could apply to the Peace Corps.

I took the applications home and explained to Cheryl all that happened. We talked most of the night discussing this possible dramatic twist in our lives. The next day, we started filling out the applications. We each wrote the required essays explaining why we wanted to serve in the Peace Corps. Both our essays were naïve, full of starry-eyed dreams of helping to make somewhere in the world a better place.

We mailed the applications and waited anxiously to find out if we had been accepted. The Peace Corps does an in-depth security check of all applicants. Two months later, we received a letter saying that we had been chosen to go into training for the program in Malawi.

We quit our jobs, put what few things we had in storage, and sold our only car on a Friday. We were to leave for training the following Monday. The excitement and purpose I felt was beyond anything I knew.

Friday afternoon, I called Washington, D.C., inquiring about paying for "excess baggage" for some machinist manuals I needed to take. The desk officer replied, "Due to a political situation between Malawi and the U.S., this program has been cancelled. We are just sending out telegrams today telling our recruits not to travel to D.C. on Monday."

My anger, sadness, and despair on hearing this far exceeded the happiness of being accepted. In the following days, I made many more telephone calls to the Peace Corps. They culminated in one that led me to the office of Joe Blatchford, the national director of the Peace Corps. "Let me speak to the head of the Peace Corps," I demanded to his assistant.

"You can't," she said, "he's at a country directors' conference in Atlanta." She hung up.

I didn't quit. I started calling the major hotels in Atlanta, saying "Joe Blatchford's room, please," at first to no avail. But on the fourth call, I heard, "Just one moment please." Three rings later, I heard, "This is Joe." I dove headfirst into a determined, expletive-infused rant, explaining all we had given up. I ended by saying "Because of this, we are now jobless and with no car! There has to be some program I can fit into, here's my phone number." I slammed the phone down in the cradle.

Shortly after, Dale Chastain, the Peace Corps Country Director for Liberia, phoned. He had been having dinner with Joe Blatchford in his hotel room when I called. Dale invited me to join a Peace Corps rural self-help development program in Liberia, which had just started in-country training. He said my wife would be able to come and that he would figure out a position for her. He wanted us on a plane to D.C. Monday.

Cheryl and I completed training, were sworn in, and assigned to Foya Kamara, a village at the end of the road to Sierra Leone, with no electricity, no running water, no other Peace Corps volunteers, and only a minimal radio signal. It was two hundred and eighty miles "into the bush" on washboard, teeth-jarring, laterite gravel roads, slick as grease in rainy season, dry as chalk dust in dry season.

Our experiences as Peace Corps volunteers for over three years were the most memorable and life-changing of our young lives. It was the toughest job we'd ever love. We took more love away from Liberia than we could ever leave behind.

When situations seem hopeless, don't give up. Never let go of your dreams.

Phillip DeSautell, and his wife Cheryl, were volunteers in Foya Kamara, and Voinjama, Lofa County, from 1969 to 1973. Both were among the first non-college graduates accepted by the Peace Corps. Phil was in the first rural self-help development program. Cheryl developed and taught a basic home economics program for village girls. Their Peace Corps experience remains the most meaningful of fifty-five years together.

FROM SUN VALLEY TO ZORZOR CENTRAL HIGH

BY KATHLEEN COREY

"I got a C?! I've never gotten a C in my life!"

It was 1969. I was a senior at the University of Washington, preparing to become a high school English teacher.

"You have an A+ for subject matter knowledge," Roy Feldstadt, my mentor teacher, said, "but a C in classroom management."

Depressed that I'd chosen a career for which I was clearly unsuited, I spent the next five years skiing the slopes of Sun Valley, supporting myself as a waitress, bartender, bookstore clerk, and substitute teacher. After five fun but somewhat meaningless years, I decided to try teaching again and applied to the Peace Corps. After I learned I was assigned to Liberia in West Africa, I called my old mentor Roy and told him the news.

"Liberia!" he said. "I was in Group 2 in Liberia! Ask for Zorzor Central High—you'll get the experience you need."

And indeed I did. No job since has been more challenging or rewarding than my job in rural Liberia teaching high school English for seventy-five dollars a month.

Arriving in Liberia in 1975, into a world of heat and unfamiliar smells and life, I told the Peace Corps staff I wanted to teach at Zorzor Central High. They were astonished. I soon learned why.

After six weeks of in-country training and a nine-hour money-bus ride on a red dirt road, rutted from torrential rains, I arrived in Zorzor to meet the principal. I was given a schedule, a book, and student rosters. I would teach five classes a day to a roomful of mostly male students, ranging in age from fourteen to thirty. Some older students wore the uniform of first grade—pink shirt with blue shorts—having started first grade as old as sixteen because of other responsibilities, such as farming and fetching wood and water on a daily basis for their extended families. Only ten percent of the students were girls, because they were expected to do all of the housework and not allowed to attend school if they were pregnant or had children. Some girls as young as twelve-to-fourteen years old had reared children.

Calling roll, I asked the students to open their books.

"What books?" they said.

I had the only book. I tried my best to teach five classes of sixty students—three hundred students a day—without any materials other than a crumbling blackboard and a few sticks of chalk. For the next months, I wrote excerpts and exercises from the book on brown paper that I got from the local butcher. I taped them on the classroom walls. Welcome to Shakespeare, Byron, Shelley, Emerson, Thoreau, and Hemingway—the authors who would be on the all-important national exam at the end of the ninth and twelfth grades.

Trying to teach three hundred students a day without books was hard enough. A bigger problem was classroom management. I'd walk into a class that hadn't had a teacher for two hours, and the students were wound up. They ignored instructions, openly carried on conversations, wrote notes, and threw spitballs.

The curriculum didn't help. Why would students who walked six miles to and from school each day and paid for supplies their families could barely afford be interested in English and American literature? What could be further from the realities of village life, where sixty percent of babies died, and malaria and schistosomiasis were common?

One morning, I took the nine-hour money-bus ride to Monrovia and used the Peace Corps office mimeograph, a time-consuming antiquated copy machine, to create my own book of African literature and poetry. I included the works of Chinua Achebe, Wole Soyinka, and Bai T. Moore, focusing on topics of interest to my students, such as growing up in a village and the history of African slavery.

I clamped down on bad classroom behavior. Students caught cheating on a test, a common practice based on the belief that you helped your friends when they needed it, were suspended for two weeks. "Miss Corey, you were so nice last year and now you're so mean," the students said. But they had to admit they were learning, and I became a popular teacher.

My students frequently came to me for help, which oftentimes I couldn't provide. Sick babies were brought to me to heal, and once when a student's mother in the lepers' compound became very ill, I was summoned to help. Students who had no kerosene lamps to read by would ask if they could borrow mine during testing week. I did what I could.

The work was challenging but deeply satisfying. Watching my students' eyes light up as they discussed issues important to them and knowing that I had helped Liberian families during some of their more difficult moments made my efforts worthwhile. I loved what I was doing so much I stayed two more years.

I received letters from my students once I returned to the States, thanking me for helping them pass the all-important national exam, as well as helping some of them with college costs. This confirmed that my four years in their community had made as profound a difference in their lives as they had in mine.

I couldn't wait to meet up with Roy to thank him for putting me on the path to a life-changing experience. Years later in my work as a refugee camp worker, NGO director, Peace Corps country director, college professor, and a diplomat, whenever I encountered a challenge, I'd remind myself that if I could teach three hundred students a day at Zorzor Central High, I could probably do just about anything.

Kathleen Corey was a Peace Corps volunteer in Zorzor and volunteer leader from 1975 to 1979. She is currently the President of Women of Peace Corps Legacy. She also served as Peace Corps country director for North Macedonia and Sri Lanka, regional director of Asia and Pacific, chief of operations for Pacific, Asia, Central and Eastern Europe, and a diplomat and NGO leader.

PEACE CORPS TRAINING

BY ELIZABETH ROBERTS THOMAS

I had recently graduated from Harpur College (now SUNY Binghamton in New York State) in July 1964. I knew I didn't want to work in a little office, like at IBM, which was hiring close to my home. My close friend Bobbie Walsh had just applied to the Peace Corps, and the idealism of JFK's words still rang in my ears. I began to give the idea of joining the Peace Corps serious thought. So, I filled out my own Peace Corps application.

My father had recently died after a long, painful illness, and I was the last of three children left at home. My mother was not at all happy about my decision. But, about a month later, I received a letter. I was going to Liberia!

We had what I think was the best Peace Corps training ever. October 1964, I was off to California. I was nervous, excited, and a bit scared. This was my first time on a plane—a huge Pan American aircraft with only eight passengers on board. One of them, it turned out, was in the same volunteer training group as I was. We had fun chatting about what might lie in the future for us.

We arrived in San Francisco. All of the new volunteers were housed at the Seal Rock Inn, a nice motel overlooking the Pacific Ocean. We attended classes at San Francisco State College for nine weeks. The program, "WACAS," was very academic. I've forgotten what all of the letters stood for, but I remember World Affairs and African Studies. We also had physical fitness classes and lectures about health, health care, and all the frightening diseases we could get in Africa: malaria, skin fungi, schistosomiasis, and others. We were given the myriad of shots necessary for our lives in the tropics.

After nine weeks in San Francisco, we were bussed off to the Sierra Nevada mountains to spend a week in a cold, rainy environment meant to "test our mettle." We divided into groups and set up our campsites. We took on various tasks like travailing a monkey bridge and killing chickens, plucking their feathers, and cooking them for dinner. That was not so much fun. Our group got one of the members who had previously killed a chicken to "whack" the chicken, while the rest of us volunteered to cook it for dinner. (I never had to kill a chicken in Liberia.) But the classes at San Francisco State and the week in the mountains led to a comradery that for many of us has lasted a lifetime.

Before leaving the U.S., we had home leave for Christmas and New Years'. In early January, we went to the Virgin Islands. Our group was split up between St. Croix and St. Thomas. The Peace Corps assigned twenty of us to teach in the various schools on the island of St. Thomas. Two of us taught in an elementary school that was formerly a hospital when the island was owned by the Dutch—a solid brick building with large, open windows that let in the cool ocean breezes.

Our "camp" was the old Civilian Conservation Corps (CCC) buildings on the other side of the mountains from the school in the capital city, Charlotte Amalie. The structures were old, tired wood, and the screens on the windows and the walls teemed with cute little beige lizards, almost translucent in color. Mosquitoes were a problem, and we were quite a treat for them. The outhouses that came with the buildings reminded me of growing up on our rural property before my parents installed working plumbing in our house. I loved riding back-and-forth to school in the rented, open air, canopy-topped jeeps.

We went to the school five days a week, doing our best to learn the skill of teaching. School started around seven-thirty in the morning and lasted until lunchtime at eleven-thirty. I worked with a first-grade teacher in the elementary school. I guessed that the Peace Corps administration thought that teaching in the Virgin Islands would be similar to teaching in Liberia. That was a bit of a reach. In Liberia, I found only two similarities: learning by rote and a rap on the knuckles by the Liberian teacher when a student didn't know the lesson. (That was a shock to me the first time I saw the teacher do this to a cute little first-grader. I wanted to yell out, "stop!" But, of course, I couldn't.)

Some days at the school in St. Thomas we were invited to eat lunch with the children. It was fun to chatter with them and trade stories about our lives. Afternoons were usually unscheduled time when we often went to the beach. We lived close to Magens Bay, one of the most uncrowded, beautiful beaches I had ever seen. Evenings, if we didn't have chores, we went back into Charlotte Amalie to socialize in local bars (I remember The Castaways as the best) with friends in our group, islanders, or sometimes members of the Navy Underwater Demolition Team (which became the Navy Seals) who were training in the waters off the shores of the islands.

One of the few disconcerting things about our training was the process of "deselection," which hung over all of us. Every now and then, someone in our group would not be there any longer. We were quietly told that suddenly the person had left the group; we were never told why and we never knew if we might be next.

Four weeks later, our training over, we flew to Puerto Rico for a three-hour stopover to buy whatever supplies we thought we might need, then to JFK to say goodbye to family. That night, we boarded an evening flight to Liberia.

We were on our way.

Elizabeth (Liz) Roberts Thomas served in the Peace Corps from 1965 to 1966 in Monrovia. After, she worked for the Office of Economic Opportunity, recruited for the Peace Corps and earned a master's in education. She taught in New York City, then moved upstate, where she and her husband taught and raised their three children. Retired, they now live in Greensboro, N.C.

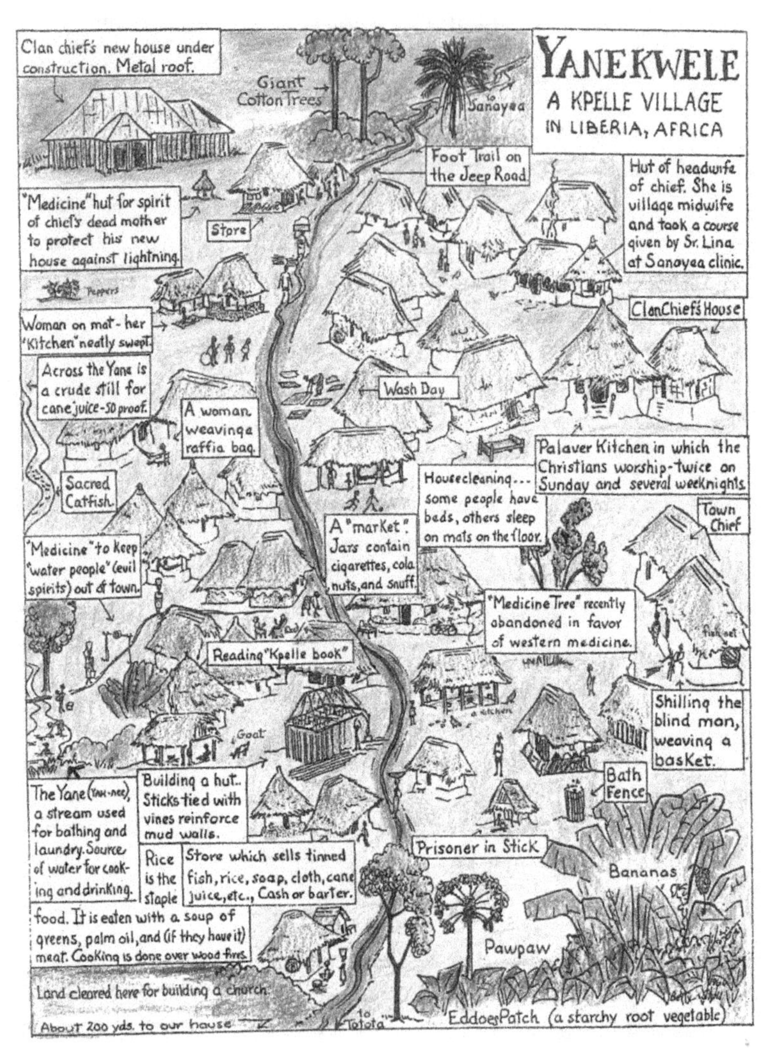

Drawing by Betty Stull Schaffer

A MISSIONARY EXPERIENCE

BY BETTY STULL SCHAFFER

There was no Peace Corps when I arrived in Liberia in 1959 with my physician-husband and our four young children. We were Lutheran missionaries and our church had worked in Liberia for a hundred years. Our first assignment was to learn the Kpelle language that had been recently translated into a written form by a linguist. With this achievement, the Kpelle people could read the Bible, write, and read news and health bulletins published in their own language. We met the linguist and his wife during our year at the School of Missions in Hartford, Connecticut. Their enthusiasm and stories were a positive introduction to Liberia.

We spent nine months living near the village of Yanekwele, which could be reached only by jeep on a difficult road. In the rainy season, bridges washed out. We were the only white family and lived seven miles from any other missionaries. Most of the villagers spoke only Kpelle. We learned a lot about their lives. It was the most interesting time in all of our eleven years in Liberia.

Working with the Kpelle people was a great way to get to know them. We hired boys to carry water from the stream and pour it into the metal drum that supplied running water to our house. Others helped me in the kitchen. A blind woman farmed rice beside our yard, and we observed the cut-and-burn method of farming. She wanted work, so she swept the dirt yard around our mud-walled house. Bare dirt discouraged snakes. We Americans, of course, had grass lawns and I was told to shuffle when I walked through grass to warn the snakes. I still find myself doing this in America.

In 1960, we moved to Zorzor, a town two hundred miles upcountry. My husband worked at the small hospital there. I heard that the house across the road had been rented to an American and his family. I was surprised to learn it was my first cousin, Don Kessler. Don told me he was in charge of a group of young men to test the possibility of a new program that the U.S. government called the Peace Corps.

In 1962, the first Peace Corps volunteers arrived in Liberia to work in education, agriculture, rural development, and health education. Their mission was to promote world peace and friendship by supplying the needed skills and improving cross-cultural understanding between the host country and America.

Through the years, the Lutheran mission and other denominations built churches, schools, clinics, and hospitals and were welcomed by the Liberian government. The goal was to care for those in need and teach Christianity. My husband helped with the planning and building of a new modern hospital near Suakoko, located a hundred miles closer to Monrovia. It was named Phebe Hospital. Our family moved to Suakoko in 1965 when the hospital was dedicated. The freed slaves who settled in Liberia chose the motto, "The love of liberty brought us here." It seemed appropriate that Phebe Hospital chose the motto "The love of Jesus brought us here."

The motivation of both the missionaries and the volunteers was similar in a basic way—to improve the lives of the people in Liberia through better health and education. There were differences. The volunteers came for a two-year term of service. Missionaries had four-year terms and often a lifetime commitment.

The Peace Corps volunteers and the missionaries also differed in their living conditions. The volunteers lived among the villagers, while missionaries lived on compounds. The volunteers were given a small stipend to pay for rent, food, and necessities. When volunteers completed their service, they received an adjustment allowance to help with resettlement back home. Missionaries were provided with salaries and maintained a lifestyle similar to what they were accustomed back home. Volunteers traveled by taxi or money-buses, while the missionaries had a fleet of vehicles and an airplane.

U.S. government agencies labeled Liberia a "hardship post." Some expatriates based in the capital of Monrovia rarely ventured upcountry to learn how the Liberians there lived. It bothered me to hear some of them criticize or ridicule the Liberians. I was privileged to live upcountry and become closer to many local villagers. I visited them in their thatched huts and on their farms and learned about their lives.

Some Peace Corps volunteers and missionary families socialized and became friends. One day my husband came home and asked if a young Peace Corps volunteer could live with us. She was sick and neither the village nor the hospital was the best place for her. Without hesitation, we took her in. When her parents came to visit from Massachusetts, we became friends. When we returned to the States, that same family helped us find a home.

We saw many Peace Corps volunteers come and go during our eleven years in Liberia. Their ages ranged from nineteen to seventy. Most were in their twenties. They all had a desire to help Liberians. The Peace Corps is about people helping people. Even today, after multiple evacuations of volunteers due to two civil wars, Ebola, AIDS, and the COVID-19 pandemic, many Liberians still remember the special Peace Corps volunteer assigned to their village.

I am now ninety-five years old and have precious memories of Liberia—similar to the volunteers. I still communicate with people I know there, thanks to the modern technology of the cell phone. Securing food, clean water, health care, and an income is still a day-to-day struggle for most Liberians.

There is no way to measure what the Peace Corps has meant to the volunteers and the people they served. I hope the Peace Corps will continue to spread understanding and goodwill. It really can build a foundation for world peace.

Betty Stull Schaffer was raised in Ohio and graduated from Wittenberg University. She spent eleven years in Liberia as a missionary wife raising her six children. At age ninety-five, she Zooms with her children weekly and talks by cell phone with her Liberian friends. Her love of painting and drawing enriched her experience of Liberia and continues to keep her busy.

AN AMERICAN TEENAGER IN LIBERIA

BY DIANE TROMBETTA

My first memory of Liberia is of a huge, shiny, brownish-black cockroach. Not a live one, but one that Dad brought home to California in 1954 to show my sister, Margo, and me. He had moved to Monrovia to build a Caterpillar Tractor dealership and supply heavy machinery for Liberia's iron ore mines, rubber plantations, and road building. He described "giant" mosquitos and having to sleep under big white nets, and how all the vegetables he ate were frozen because it was too hot and humid to grow tomatoes or lettuce. He said there weren't many foreign families there because they got sick from the tropical diseases and there weren't enough schools and houses, but the beaches were beautiful, and the soil was bright red. My sister and I thought his life sounded dangerous, exotic, and exciting.

My next memory of Liberia is a bowl of oatmeal in my dad's Monrovia kitchen in 1959. I was thirteen. Our prop plane had flown into Robertsfield late at night. We were exhausted, thrilled to see our dad, and excited to be in a new country. He took us to his modern concrete-block house on Mamba Point overlooking the ocean. While we unpacked, he cooked oatmeal for us, apologizing that it was made with canned milk because there was no fresh milk in Monrovia stores. It was the best oatmeal I have ever tasted. The next morning, we drove downtown. Remembering that ride, I recall red, iron-rich dirt roads, little storefronts along a main street, small houses under corrugated metal roofs, and bare-breasted women balancing huge baskets on their heads as they walked gracefully along the roadside. (Later, Dad told me the missionaries were working hard to convince rural women to cover their breasts.) I had lived in Africa during elementary school but in a country with a dry Mediterranean climate—Algeria. I felt the oppressive humidity as we drove the streets of Monrovia. I recall looking down at my arm and seeing a large, bright red mosquito bite. *I really am in the tropics,* I thought. I wondered if the bite was going to get infected.

So began my three years in Liberia. I don't have dramatic stories to tell, but I do have memories of a unique time and place and experiences that shaped my life.

I wasn't bothered by being the only Caucasian at the Monrovia Demonstration School (junior high) and later at the College of West Africa (high school). My Liberian classmates were either friendly or just ignored me. I made friends with two Liberian girls and liked all my teachers. Mr. Okpala was a tall, elegant-looking man with a mild British accent. He had been educated in the U.K. and taught Latin. I wondered how Latin would be of any use to me, much less to my Liberian classmates. My biology teacher had earned her bachelor's degree in the U.S. Her classes were standard Biology 101 until the day she told us she knew a woman in her village who could change herself into a leopard. I was mystified how, with a college degree in biology, she could believe in the leopard woman myth. Then I remembered that there were plenty of people in the U.S. with science degrees who believed in angels.

Monrovia was a mini United Nations. From my teenage perspective, adults and children from different countries seemed to mingle effortlessly. The children of professionals, small business owners, building contractors, and diplomats from Europe, the Middle East, and the U.S. came to Monrovia to "develop" the country. I partied at local dance halls with Liberian teenagers. My best friend, Samira, was a Lebanese girl whose family owned a small market. I taught her how to make American apple pie and she taught me how to make *kofte.* My sister had a huge crush on Kiki, the son of the Swedish consul, and her best friend was from Belgium. Liberians taught us about Highlife music, and everybody danced together. No one worried about skin color.

Living in Liberia was like living in a greenhouse. Plants flourished. We had a gladiola in full bloom just ten days after planting the bulb. Bacteria and parasites loved the climate too. I remember the beautiful blue-purple color of the disinfectant in the water we used every day to wash our vegetables. I got intestinal worms anyway.

One of the biggest changes in my family's lifestyle was the presence of servants—from our driver, Lemuel, to our gardener, Harry, to our housekeeper, John and our cook, Jesse. These grown men were called "houseboys" and were paid about thirty dollars a month plus meals and extra rice. I thought we all got along very well, but in 1989, Liberia paid a huge price for the gap between the Americo-Liberian ruling class and the native Liberian majority they ruled.

Although today I can say that growing up in different countries gave me a global perspective I cherish, leaving good friends, switching between French and English, and trying to fit into peer groups of different nationalities came at a cost. I had trouble readjusting to life in the U.S. I felt like a fish out of water. When I returned to the U.S. in 1961 as a high school sophomore, I wasn't prepared for the cliques, the popularity contests, the rivalries and competitiveness. There was nothing cosmopolitan about high school in Palo Alto. In college, I majored in cultural anthropology. I began to understand better how exposure to different cultures had affected me; I began to appreciate the richness of my background and to make peace with my past. Maybe because I was a teenager when I lived in Liberia, or because my dream of an "intact family" seemed to come true there, or because life was so dramatically different from anything I had experienced before, my emotional connection to Liberia has remained surprisingly strong.

Today, of course, I relate to Liberia from a distance. I support her return to stability and peace by donating to Liberia-based nonprofits. I fervently wish the best for Liberia and her people, and will always be grateful for the many ways I have been enriched by living for a few years in her midst.

Diane Trombetta lived in Liberia as a teenager in the late '50s and early '60s. Her father owned Libtraco, a CAT tractor dealership that supplied heavy machinery for Liberia's roads, rubber plantations, and iron mines. She attended local public schools and became part of a community of Liberians and expatriates from various parts of Europe and the Middle East.

BEATING RICE

BY BETTY STULL SCHAFFER

Gillima and Lingbing . . .
The blind woman and her daughter,
Beating rice in a wooden mortar.
Thud . . . thud . . . thud . . . thud
Two long sticks coming down on country rice.
Thud . . . thud . . . thud . . . thud
The heavy sticks are lifted high.
First Gillima's stick and then Lingbing's,
Up . . . down . . . up . . . down
Thud . . . thud . . . thud . . . thud.

Gillima has a vague smile,
Her eyes are blue-white, sightless.
Yet her stick never misses the mortar.
Thud . . . thud . . . thud . . . thud
Lingbing's slender body moves rhythmically;
Her arms are strong, her skirt swinging.
The hot sun sends warmth over everything.
I watch them work together
Who would guess that Gillima is sightless?
Thud . . . thud . . . thud . . . thud.

An eye infection when she was young
Was treated with hot pepper!
Now they know it was a mistake.
Westerners bring useful knowledge.
The Liberians teach us the importance of a community
Accepting and supporting a blind person.
Gillima carries water, fetches firewood, farms the fields,
Sweeps the yard, and cares for her son and daughter.
Sometimes she needs to be led,
Other times her bare feet feel the path.

Peace Corps volunteers have told me
That their experiences changed them forever.
As a missionary's wife I, too, am changed by
My eleven years in Liberia.
Seeing Gillima and Lingbing beating rice
Speaks both to my seeing eyes and my heart.
Quiet fills the thatch kitchen behind them.
There is PEACE here.
Thud . . . thud . . . thud . . . thud.
Thud . . . thud . . . thud . . . thud.

Betty Stull Schaffer was raised in Ohio and graduated from Wittenberg University. She spent eleven years in Liberia as a missionary wife raising her six children. At age ninety-five, she Zooms with her children weekly and talks by cell phone with her Liberian friends. Her love of painting and drawing enriched her experience of Liberia and continues to keep her busy.

Drawing by Betty Stull Schaffer

IF YOU REALLY WANT TO BE OF SERVICE

BY CURRAN ROLLER

When I arrived in Liberia in December 1982, I trained with all the other education volunteers at Cuttington University in Suacoco until February 1983. About two-thirds of the way through training, each of us visited our intended site for several days to learn what we could, meet key people, and return to complete the training.

I journeyed to Sasstown, a small fishing village on the coast about as far as one could get from Monrovia, the capital city. During a four-day stay, I met the principal of the public school, who would become my boss. I saw the stick-and-mud house where I would live and visited the beautiful beach. I met the Catholic missionaries who ran a small medical clinic in town and observed how people lived and worked. The thing that surprised me most was the absence of a food store or outdoor market. People obtained food through a complex, word-of-mouth system that included hunters, fishermen, farmers, and bakers. If someone shot a deer, baked some bread, harvested some rice, or produced food in any way, I would have to get on the "network" to be able to buy some.

On day four, I visited the home of Mr. Blidi, the district education officer. Mr. Blidi was the most powerful government official in Grand Kru County. I would need his support to succeed in my primary teaching assignment as well as my secondary project to coordinate teacher development events. A lot was riding on this first meeting, so I was very excited and keyed up. It was somewhat disappointing to learn that Mr.

Blidi wasn't home—last-minute Ministry of Education business had called him away. Of course, Liberian hospitality required that Mrs. Blidi should invite me in and serve tea and light snacks. We went into the living room with some relatives and sat down.

While sitting in the living room, I noticed that the household seemed to be in a state of commotion. I heard wailing and animated conversation coming from the back of the house. I asked Mrs. Blidi if I could help with whatever the matter was. At first, she didn't want to say, but the relatives implored her to tell the story. They seemed to be angry with Mrs. Blidi for some reason. Mrs. Blidi was desperately concerned about her young son who was running quite a high fever—already one hundred and three degrees and climbing. I asked if the clinic was closed, at which point, the relatives' disapproval of Mrs. Blidi became clear: she was refusing to take the boy to the clinic on religious grounds. Along with friends and relatives from her church, Mrs. Blidi had been praying over her son for the past two days. The people in the household were divided into two camps and everyone was angry. Just as I was about to get mad, lose control, and yell out my opinion, I remembered what the Liberian trainers had been teaching us: "If you try to boss people around and act like a know-it-all American, no one will listen to you, and you won't be able to help anyone."

Instead of talking, I listened and asked questions. "Which church do you attend?" "Did the pastor say that people shouldn't go to doctors?" "What did you hear or read that led to your decision to rely on prayer only?" Her answers made it clear that avoiding medical help was not necessarily the canon in her church, but rather her interpretation of what she had read about God's provisional nature and the importance of prayer. It also became clearer that the relatives who disagreed with Mrs. Blidi were on her husband's side of the family. Had Mr. Blidi been home, the decision would have been his. They reasoned that he would have taken the boy to the clinic, being a modern man who believed in science.

Mrs. Blidi seemed confident that the pastor would agree with her, but I wasn't so sure. There was a child's life at stake, so a risk had to be taken. I asked Mrs. Blidi if we could go to the pastor's house together and let the pastor's opinion be the deciding one. She agreed, and what ensued was like something out of a movie: a parade of relatives followed Mrs. Blidi and me to the home of the pastor, arguing all the way. Luckily, the pastor said, "Take that child to the clinic immediately!" Mrs. Blidi actually seemed relieved. I think she wanted a doctor for her son but felt constrained by her religious beliefs. Now that religious authority aligned with her maternal instincts, she seemed happy to go to the clinic for help.

I had to leave the next day, so I didn't find out until later that the missionaries at the clinic got the Blidis' son all fixed up with a simple malaria shot. When I returned to Sasstown after training, Mr. Blidi threw a feast for me like I was his long lost son. Mrs. Blidi treated me like a friend who had helped her out of a tight spot, and the community in general welcomed me and supported my work over the next two years.

This episode made some fundamental Peace Corps' training axioms very concrete for me: If you want to be of help, don't come into the situation spouting opinions and giving orders. Instead, listen first to people's concerns. Seek solutions that honor people's views and wishes—don't ignore them. Always look for ways to build relationships with other people, not ways to be "right" at the cost of someone else being wrong. Over the next two years, many other experiences would confirm the value of these lessons. Not only were these principles critical to my success while working in Liberia, I never forgot them. Over a thirty-year career in teaching, they have guided me and stay with me to this day.

Curran Roller was a Peace Corps volunteer in Sasstown, Grand Kru County, from 1983 to 1985, and taught math in Sasstown High School. Curran later acquired his master's degree in education and worked in the Fairfax County school system for twenty-nine years. Curran enjoys traveling with his wife, Nora, playing pickleball with son, Nick, and visiting family in California every summer.

THE OLD MAN AND THE SEA

BY LARRY R. EATON

In 1968, early during my six-week training period in Harper on Liberia's southernmost tip, I met an old man. He lived with his wife in a simple home immediately behind the house where I lived with several other teachers. The old man told me he was a Kru fisherman. He quickly won my respect.

While I had recently received my law degree and deemed myself to be reasonably well-educated and well-versed in my native tongue of English, foreign languages had long stumped me: Latin had defeated me in high school, French did the same in college, and my efforts during this training period to grapple with Grebo, the principal language in Maryland County where Cape Palmas (Harper) was located, were to be proving equally unsuccessful. In stark contrast, my new friend was fully fluent in at least four languages: Kru, his native language, Grebo, English, and French (logically, given the proximity of Côte d'Ivoire, where French was universally spoken).

Our new friendship was cemented when I offered the old fisherman my used razor blades. In those days, I shaved with double-edged Gillette "blue blades," which became dull after being used a significant number of times. I do not think that his enthusiastic appreciation for receiving my used razor blades could have been greater had they been made of gold.

My new friend described his livelihood: His daily ritual was to depart in the early morning, before the sun was up, in his little two-man canoe (which he pronounced "kay-noo"). His "tackle," such as it was, was a stout line, a sturdy hook, and perhaps, some sort of bait. He would row his boat far out into the ocean to a location that his experience told him was best. There, he would cast his line. He had neither rod and reel, nor pole. If he had a strike on his line, he would haul it in, hand-over-hand. At day's end, he would row his canoe back home with his catch for the day.

One evening, my new friend came to my house looking for me. He wanted me to come to the market to see his catch for that day. The "market," in this case, was a vacant lot perhaps a hundred yards down the road. I went with him, and there, lying on a sheet, I saw two huge sharks, side-by-side. Each measured well over six feet in length and certainly weighed well over a hundred pounds apiece. I believed one was a blue shark; the other, unmistakably, was a hammerhead.

It was then that I first noticed my friend's thickly callused hands. His palms had been cut to shreds. I asked how he had possibly managed to bring back even one of these sharks, let alone two.

He told me this story: After winning his battle with the first shark, he had to get it into the canoe so that it would not be attacked and torn apart by other sharks that infested the area. To do that, he had to dive overboard, hoist the shark up, and push it into his boat. Having accomplished that, rather than returning home, he kept fishing and landed a second shark. Obviously, to get the second shark into the boat, he had to follow the same procedure as with the first shark. By then, the little boat was so small that the two sharks completely filled it. So, the old man had to swim back home, through shark-infested waters, pulling his canoe and catch behind him.

Having managed to get his two sharks back to market, my friend would now sell the meat. The proceeds, even at pennies a pound, would support his family for quite some time.

After our training in Harper came to an end and I moved to Monrovia, I never saw my friend again. But I have thought of him often. I am certain that his hands healed. His calluses hardened again. Within a few days, he was once again up before dawn, rowing far out into the Atlantic in his two-man canoe. Heading for where he knew he would find sharks. Casting his hook and line. Battling his catch, hand-over-hand. Living his life, as he had always done.

Larry R. Eaton was a Peace Corps volunteer in Monrovia from 1968 to 1970. He taught at the law school at the University of Liberia. In addition, he counseled an orphanage, helped coach a boys' high school basketball team, and participated in an amateur acting group. After that, Larry practiced law for forty-four years. He and his wife live in Chicago, Illinois.

ASK NOT . . .

BY ELIZABETH ROBERTS THOMAS

Nobody got any sleep on our all-night flight to Liberia. After a quick lay-over in Senegal, we landed at Robertsfield—Liberia's only international airport, southeast of the capital city of Monrovia. It was our first real taste of the hot, humid, tropical air. We were quickly ushered through customs, then warmly greeted by Peace Corps and Liberian officials. After short, welcoming speeches, we boarded two yellow, mud-splattered buses and headed to Monrovia. Along the route, we tried to take in everything so vividly new. Local women in brightly colored, long, straight skirts and bright tops (we later learned were called *lappas*) carried large pots or baskets on their heads and babies on their backs swaddled in cloth, postures so erect and bundles carefully balanced. Men wore tattered T-shirts and shorts while walking in the blazing sun, some herded a few goats. A breeze swayed the palm trees in the hot, almost suffocating air.

We arrived in early February 1965. We were teachers, enthusiastic about getting our assignments. However, the Liberian school year did not start for another month. Now, we were on Liberian time, and this was our first challenging lesson. Eager to "get going," it seemed everyone else was moving slowly, so slowly.

We filled the time exploring Monrovia, learning about the shops and restaurants, helping with typing for the library, doing paperwork for the Voice of America, a U.S.-based international radio station, and, most importantly, learning how to navigate local travel. The two main modes of transportation were either taking a taxi or flagging down the "money-bus," a large van with the back open and benches on either side that passengers hopped on and off whenever it stopped. We quickly learned to be prepared for anyone or anything to be on the seat next to us, frequently sharing it with mothers nursing their babies, big bundles on the floor, and maybe even a few chickens. Passengers yelled "Ya!" to the driver when someone wanted to stop, paid their five cents, and hopped off.

February crawled; I wanted to learn where I would be assigned. Others in my group, little by little, received assignments to their schools in different parts of the country. They excitedly chatted with friends about where they were going, started collecting supplies, and headed out of the city to settle into their new homes.

Finally, the "assignment people" called me in. They told me I was to teach music at Methodist Elementary in Monrovia.

Teach music!

My idea of "roughing it" in a small village and teaching in a welcoming school where I was desperately needed quickly vanished.

"It couldn't be!"

I had requested an upcountry assignment. Almost all my friends in my group were going to different rural villages. I thought I would be, too. They explained that I had received this assignment because I was a music major in college. Yes, I had attended a liberal arts college. As a music major, all I needed were twenty-five hours of music history and music theory. I played the clarinet and the piano, but I knew nothing about teaching music. However, I was the only one in our group that had "music major" in my paperwork.

Depression threatened to swallow me. The image of what my Peace Corps experience was supposed to be was shattered. I thought maybe I should just quit and go home. But I remembered President Kennedy's words, still so clear in my head, "Ask not . . ." I joined the Peace Corps to do something for my country; maybe things would make sense eventually.

As I learned more about my assignment, it started to make more sense to me, and my outlook became more positive. Under the principalship of Dr. Brown, a cultured, well-educated missionary and close friend of President William Tubman, the school had worked hard to raise money for musical instruments, which had recently arrived. The Peace Corps volunteer assigned to teach music and direct the band had fallen sick and returned to the U.S., leaving the school desperately in need of a music teacher. Maybe I could do some good! And so, I stayed.

The following two years were an incredible experience. I taught music to all grade levels in the school cafeteria before classroom lessons began. Every day, the room filled with children's voices ringing out across the open space, their hands clapping in rhythm as we sang newly learned songs. I learned about African music and taught them as much as possible while sharing my growing collection of African instruments. During the day, I started teaching instrumental lessons, and when the children were ready, we started band practice. I was so proud of the children's work, practicing and playing as a group as we prepared for our concerts.

The parents raised money to buy material and sewed blue-and-gold uniforms. We performed for our school's Christmas concert and were the musical support for the production of "Hansel and Gretel." Additionally, we had a recital on the Liberian television station and an appearance at the Liberian Red Cross concert at the University of Liberia. Our school also invited President Tubman to an evening celebration for his birthday, and our band played and sang for him.

Elizabeth (second from left) with her teacher colleagues, 1965

I took many trips upcountry to visit friends, some in small towns and some in rural villages. My roommate, Barbara (Brown) Kennedy, was another Peace Corps volunteer. We hosted many of our friends at our apartment when they visited Monrovia and had fun sharing experiences and Liberian "chop" dinners.

During our month-long school break in February, we went to East Africa: Kenya, Uganda, and Tanzania. It was an opportunity for me to explore a whole new world, which might have been impossible if I had not stayed in my Peace Corps assignment.

Although I was anxious to get home when my two years ended, I was heartbroken about leaving all the wonderful people I had known in Liberia. Very special and happy memories of Liberia's gracious and generous hospitality stay with me still, almost sixty years later!

Elizabeth (Liz) Roberts Thomas served in the Peace Corps from 1965 to 1966 in Monrovia. She then worked for the Office of Economic Opportunity, recruited for the Peace Corps, and earned a master's in education. She taught in New York City, then moved upstate, where she and her husband taught and raised their three children. Retired, they live now in Greensboro, N.C.

ZORZOR, LIBERIA: ONE HEALTH . . . ONE WORLD

BY KAREN HEIN, MD

As a twenty-five-year-old, fourth-year medical student from Columbia University's College of Physicians in New York, I arrived in the fall of 1969 to spend my two-month elective in upcountry Liberia. It was my "Peace Corps equivalent" experience, since it was the only time I could carve out in my burgeoning medical career. I thought I was coming to learn about diseases and treatments. And I did, when upon arrival I ran directly into a measles epidemic in the villages around Zorzor. People filled Curran Hospital—the nearest place with medical staff and equipment to care for the many seriously ill. Each bed was surrounded by families who slept on the floor next to the patients, feeding, bathing, and nurturing their loved ones. With the hospital packed with patients and families, there weren't enough nurses and only one doctor to administer the needed health care. Patients ranged in age from newborn infants to the elderly, many of whom were dying from measles complications, such as pneumonia and encephalitis.

During my first day, I was introduced to Dr. Paul Mertens, the only physician serving as part of the Lutheran Mission. His calm demeanor, coupled with his constant motion, made him seem omnipresent as he moved from making rounds on the patients, to being the surgeon in the operating room, often lit by a kerosene lantern when the generator was down. Dr. Mertens wrote a four-by-six-inch reference guide for me containing the common illnesses, parasitic, and bacterial infections that we were able to treat with our limited supplies. The card contained the name of the medication, dose, condition or diagnosis, plus the cost of treatment: fifteen cents for a daily treatment for hookworm or ascaris worms; four dollars for a fourteen-day course of tablets to treat Onchocerciasis volvulus (the cause of "river blindness"). I carried this card with me wherever I went on the hospital grounds, on vaccination treks through the jungle, and on short flights to reach more isolated communities.

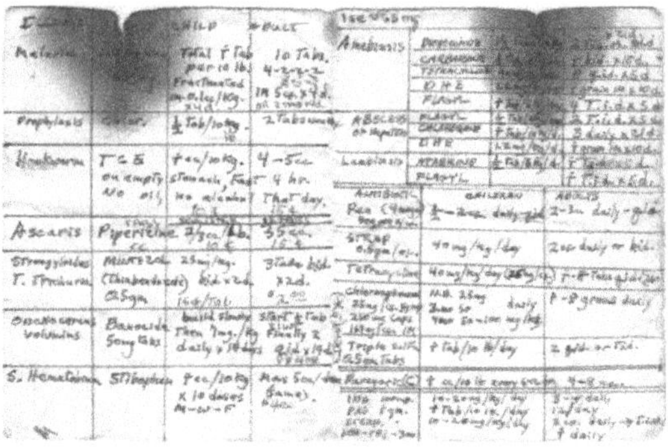

Hand-written, 4x6 medical reference guide

Dr. Mertens knew everything about each person. The X-ray machine produced images that had to be read immediately before the ever-present mildew and mold would turn their images of lungs or broken bones into a picture of opaque fern patterns, making it impossible to read. Local nursing students helped teach family members how to care for their loved ones. The need for many more hands in the midst of the measles epidemic was critical, because the care was more than we could possibly handle.

Then, I met Nurse Esther Bacon, in whose house I would be living. Others told me she was a legend because she created a school of nursing for young women who came from ten surrounding communities speaking different local languages. (I would later find a book dedicated to Ester: *Outlaw For God: The Story of Esther Bacon* by J. Birney Dibble, The Christopher Publishing House, Hanover, MA, 1992.) Esther would wake me up in the middle of the night to join her at a difficult delivery or to assist with a crisis that couldn't wait for the light of day. She never seemed to sleep. Esther showed me the two crowded rooms with about ten beds, but not enough for everyone. About fifteen more patients lay on floor mats. One room was for children and the other one was for adults.

In my short two-month assignment, I lived closely with the land, negotiating the rainy season's muddy trails and swollen rivers. We all lived adjacent to the animals that provided peppery wild bush meat meals that also turned out to be the source of emerging infections like Lassa fever and Ebola. Sadly, just three years after I lived with her, Esther Bacon died in 1972 of Lassa fever, one of the first people diagnosed with this previously unknown illness contracted from living in close proximity to infected rats. We lived in a village with thatch-roofed homes and ever-present fires for cooking food. Thirteen-foot pythons lived in the surrounding bush and we had to use a flashlight at night when walking from our home to the hospital to avoid stepping on poisonous snakes. Malaria and other endemic, insect-borne illnesses, as well as teeth abscesses and injuries, were all part of life in upcountry Lofa County. People sought care for these illnesses often after trying traditional healing practices. I once traded a tube of antibiotic ointment for a bee's-wax-wrapped amulet when a villager thought they would try our medicine instead of the village healer's offering. Often both approaches were combined as a "win-win" solution for many people.

Karen providing vaccinations

I learned about how disease-related beliefs dictated what actions people would choose. I learned about how family members could be taught to save their babies' lives when infants suffered from tetanus by having their mothers learn how to "gavage" (insert a small feeding tube into the stomach of the baby) to keep the tiny one nourished until the muscle tightness preventing breast feeding could be relieved. I learned that over time, peoples' reluctance to come to the hospital could be reversed when they were greeted by nurses from their own villages working so closely with the beloved and deeply respected nurse, Esther Bacon, and Dr. Paul Mertens.

We made regular visits to nearby villages by trekking through the jungle terrain, wading through rivers, or flying a lightweight plane into more remote areas where Peace Corps volunteers lived. We vaccinated the villagers for the preventable diseases of polio, tetanus, diphtheria, pertussis, and measles that Liberians had come to know and were increasingly willing and able to prevent. The powerful messages of how to help people create a healthy environment, immunizing to prevent deadly illnesses, and the ability of families to be caregivers were the experiences imprinted on my mind, my spirit, and my soul.

I learned much from Liberians and those early years in Zorzor. Now, as the COVID pandemic has affected the world, I've learned how the Liberians have readily followed masking as a preventive intervention and about their readiness to receive the vaccine as it becomes available. Liberia learned about the power of vaccines that could prevent measles over fifty years ago . . . being among them shaped my medical career at the most impressionable time in my medical education.

Zorzor was my place of learning. The staff at Curran Hospital were the people who taught me the importance of maintaining and regaining health. Curran Hospital was a place to go to give and receive life-enhancing skills, honoring the connection of family and community and the sense that we are *all* in this together . . . "One Health" and one world.

Karen Hein, MD, was transformed by her experience in Zorzor as a medical student in 1969. During the next five decades, she worked in global health and equity, in academia and philanthropy, at the National Academy of Medicine, and for the Vermont state and federal governments. She shepherds an American Cashmere Goat herd and loves fiber arts, photography, and indigo shibori dyeing. Find out more about Karen at www.karenhein.com.

SILENT MOVIE

BY AUSTIN LAVOIE

I went to Liberia as a teacher in 1965. I was assigned to a school that was a large, one-room classroom where all the teachers could overhear one another in their class groups.

One day, the principal showed me a place where a school had been started about ten years before, but for some reason, construction had stopped. All the walls were up, but they had mildew on them and were overgrown with weeds. I had a little construction experience, and it looked to me as if the building just needed a concrete floor and a tin roof.

I knew the United States Agency for International Development (USAID) would donate materials for schools if the town showed an interest. In a roundabout way, Webbo, Grand Gedeh County, was not run by the village chief as was typical. Instead, Webbo was run by the principal of the school. He was a man of few words, but he got things accomplished fast. If I needed sand to be brought to the school, *Boom!*, it was done. Even though the kids carried the sandbags half a mile from the river to the school, no one complained.

The principal and I thought that a good way for the town to show interest was to raise money to hire skilled help. We had four men in mind: two strong masons and two strong boys. Meanwhile, the principal would send all the unskilled help I needed, which was mainly school kids assisting with the project.

I needed a way to draw the townspeople in. I decided to show a movie. There was a small, old generator in the middle of town that could turn on a light bulb if someone needed a little light after dark for one reason or another.

I asked USAID if I could borrow a movie projector. Then, I asked the movie theater owner in nearby Harper if I could borrow a movie. He gave me *The Steel Helmet*, which was about a small group of men fighting in the Korean War.

The crowd started to file into the room, and I soon had a full house, maybe fifty people. All the windows were jam-packed with faces of patrons watching from outside for free. The admission price was only ten cents in U.S. dollars.

I started the generator and ran an extension cord into my theater, which was the school. I turned on the projector and began to show the movie—no sound. I turned a switch, and it had sound, but there was no picture. I wished I had practiced before it was showtime.

Ultimately, I decided to show the movie without sound. I thought it was going to be a flop. However, the crowd filled in with all the sound effects I needed—wailing, cheering, and laughing—throughout the movie. They really seemed to have a good time. I think they enjoyed the movie more without the sound.

Unsure of how many people paid that day, I told USAID we raised seventy-five U.S. dollars (fifty of which came from my pocket) to hire skilled help. USAID came through with all the required concrete plus tin for the roof. We used a Peace Corps jeep to haul the materials to the site from Harper.

About six months later, we had a new school. My kind of construction experience, the kind that required electricity and concrete trucks, just did not work on this side of the world. There had been only one way to build it—the Liberian way. And it started with a silent movie.

Austin Lavoie was a Peace Corps volunteer in Liberia from 1965 to 1968 and worked as a teacher in Webbo, Grand Gedeh County. He also worked in community development in other parts of the country. After his service, he moved to Hawaii with several other volunteers and worked in construction on Maui for the next forty years.

RAISING THE ROOF

BY JOE JAUREGUI

As a Peace Corps volunteer in Gbarnga in 1968, I was asked to be responsible for the continuing development of a basketball league among the upcountry schools. Interest in basketball had grown to the point that a tournament had been held among several schools the previous year. Gbarnga had the only gymnasium outside Monrovia, making it the perfect—and only—venue.

Two schools in Gbarnga—Gboveh High School and W.V.S. Tubman Jr. High School—already had basketball teams. Rev. Ulysses Samuel Gray and his wife, Vivienne, missionaries who served in Liberia from 1948 to 1974, had overseen the construction of the Gbarnga mission, including a combination auditorium-gymnasium building that provided the foundation for the sport. I hadn't been in town long as a Peace Corps teacher before students from a third school, St. Martin's Catholic Mission, came to my house and asked if I would be their basketball coach.

Traditionally, students wrote a "challenge" letter to neighboring schools, asking to compete in soccer, volleyball, or basketball. Whenever game day arrived, all the students would climb onto a flatbed truck in the early morning and travel to the game site. What I remember most about these excursions was riding in the back of a truck packed with students singing at the top of their lungs to the beat of a drum as we lumbered down a dusty road.

The league and the availability of the gym provided a new experience for the St. Martin's students. Twelve teams from throughout Bong, Lofa, and Nimba counties made up the league membership. Games were scheduled on Friday evenings and all day Saturdays. The gymnasium was always filled with standing-room-only crowds.

One game occurred toward the end of the first season between St. Martin's and Totota. The teams were tied in the standings and the winner of the game would earn the eighth and last berth in the tournament. Totota dominated the first half but only had a one-point lead at halftime.

As the second half began, the St. Martin's players matched their opponent basket for basket. The crowd became louder and louder. As the game progressed, with the lead constantly changing, the crowd gave a deafening roar each time St. Martin's made a basket. On several occasions following the crowd's response, I heard a loud "crack." I didn't give it much thought, assuming it was a nearby lightning strike, which often accompanied the thunderstorms that passed through on a regular basis.

At the end of regulation play, we were tied, forty-three to forty-three. We went into overtime and scored seven unanswered points to earn the victory. Afterward, outside, I realized that the ground was dry and no storm had passed through during the game. Looking to the top of the gym, I noticed the corrugated sheet metal roof and realized the loud sounds I'd heard were the metal sheets slapping against each other, lifted each time the crowd let out its deafening roar. The walls of the building were thick and the only direction the energy and noise of the crowd could go was up. The St. Martin's basketball team had literally "raised the roof."

The tournament grew in popularity for the next two decades, but was discontinued when civil conflict erupted in the late 1980s. In 2012, due to the efforts of the Liberian Youth and Sports Minister S. Tornorlah Varpilah, and several former basketball players, the tournament was reestablished. Minister Varpilah, a graduate of St. Martin's, Gboveh High School, and Cuttington University, played in the tournaments in the 1970s. His goal was to bring Liberians together through sports after years of civil war.

In 2016, Peace Corps Director for Liberia Kevin Fleming contacted Friends of Liberia. He had been approached by the Liberian Basketball Referees Association (LIBRA) requesting assistance in obtaining referee uniforms and equipment for the program. With the country recovering from the Ebola crisis, support was hard to acquire. With the assistance of the director, I was able to provide jerseys and embroidered Liberian flag patches to the referees.

In the scope of world events, basketball may not make the cut, but in Liberia, a country that has endured more than its share of calamities over the past three decades, basketball has offered a fleeting respite and an opportunity to "raise the roof."

Joe Jauregui was a Peace Corps volunteer in Gbarnga, Liberia, from 1967 to 1969. He taught at St. Martin's Catholic Mission. After that, he continued his career as an educator, serving as a teacher and administrator in Ventura County, California, for thirty-five years. He and his wife of forty-nine years raised a family and have been active as volunteers in community organizations.

Basketball referees and coaches in 2016

A BAG OF RICE

BY KATHRYN ROEN WOODWARD

I haven't eaten a grain of Liberian dryland rice in more than fifty years, yet to me it remains the one to win any blind taste test anywhere on the planet. It was that good.

Rice was our staple. In 1963, in the village of Kpain, Nimba County, we bought rice locally in hundred-pound sacks, each sack standing proudly upright in our kitchen. The rice depleted steadily day by day as it fed a pair of volunteers, three student houseboys, and the occasional visitor. Dinner was a large scoop or two topped with a sauce of finely cut greens—collards or a vegetable everyone called "potato," but which certainly was something other than the North American variety, whose leaves are toxic. Sometimes we added canned Danish hamburger patties sourced at the local Lebanese shop. And always there was a measure of hot peppers. My ration of peppers increased in tandem with the months of my tour and was something to be proud of, even if for months after I left Liberia, its fiery memory spoiled the taste of blander food. Our boys, who slept in a house across the road, made enough dinner each night to be able to pile into the kitchen before school for a leftover breakfast.

I have forgotten how long it took to empty each bag. Or how many bags we bought over the time we spent in the village. A bag always stood in attendance under the kitchen window. Always, that is, until the day we came home from school to find the spot empty.

We were aghast. It was not hard to imagine the theft. The window was not that far above the ground. It would be simple for someone tall enough to lean through and snatch the bag. But thievery was not a common occurrence in the town. At least it was not something I had heard much about, and as such, the news spread quickly. It made its way easily to the schoolhouse and into the town's warren of thatch-roofed huts, and then it ventured up our road to reach the ears of the chief.

It sent our students on a wild hunt.

"Come quick, teacher," one small boy panted, calling through the open door.

I followed him to a nearby house. It was supposedly vacant but someone had obviously been squatting there. Eager students led me through the rooms. They gleefully pointed to the sack of rice and then to my surprise, to items I hadn't noticed were missing: tins of food, a spare toothbrush still in its packaging, two water glasses, a long-outdated magazine, and a book lifted from the small, boxed library the Peace Corps provided to its volunteers. In the last room, one of the older boys reached up and ran his hands along an exposed beam. He came away with a pack of cigarettes and some matches. They were mine, but they lay in his upturned palm like an offering to me.

We took everything back home.

A day or so later, the chief came by to see the evidence. He arrived accompanied by an entourage that crowded behind him into the house. I took them into the kitchen. I indicated the bag of rice now restored to its rightful place and then I lifted a bit of drapery covering a shelf to expose the other items, the tins of food, some water glasses, a few spoons. I stated our displeasure at what had been done. The chief may have nodded in agreement. I am not sure. He did understand some English, but I spoke no Mano. He had only glanced at the smaller items. He was too busy giving his attention, his full attention, to the rice. He was silent and so were we. I even found myself holding my breath. I had no idea what was on his mind, but I knew what was on mine: that the chief's interest in canned peaches or bits of silverware was minimal because these were objects easily replaced by people like me, equipped with a monthly salary far above the earnings of almost everyone in his village. The rice, however, was more meaningful. Maybe even sacred. It was the sustenance that enabled them all—himself, the men in the room, his townsfolk—to survive. When the chief finally did speak, what I took to be a single sentence, it was answered in unison by a low murmur of agreement from his entourage. Then he turned to leave. We parted, his men and I, to make a path for him. Exiting, their plastic sandals slapped the concrete floor and raised small dust storms as they trooped off up the road toward the chief's house.

Not long after, another procession appeared. This one moved in the opposite direction. It came from the chief's compound traveling toward town. Everyone on our road came out to watch. I stood with the houseboys on our front porch. Some men who could have been among the group that recently visited were now in the khaki uniform of the Liberian National Guard. Trudging along with them was a boy of about the same age as our oldest students. They had bound his hands with rope.

"Is he the thief?" I asked those around me but got no answer.

The boy's eyes were downcast. He did not look our way as the procession reached our house, although he must have known the house somewhat intimately, having been inside to lift tins and spoons, cigarettes and the toothbrush. What he did know, what we all knew, was that his immediate future was not bright.

The boy and his escorts moved on. They now approached the fork in the road where if you turned left you came upon the schoolhouse. They turned right, toward the main road to the coast. Watching them pass out of view, I tried not to think of where they might be taking him.

Kathryn Roen Woodward was a Peace Corps volunteer in Kpain, Nimba County, from 1963 to 1965, teaching in the elementary school. After a year on her own in Africa, some of it back in Liberia, she married another Liberian volunteer. Together, they served with the Peace Corps in Micronesia, and then immigrated to Canada. She lives in Vancouver.

SASSYWOOD MAN

BY MICHAEL HOHL

I had been in-country for a little over a month and was finally being officially introduced to my boss. Sanniquellians would remark, "That man is dark-o. Fini-black." When I met Gabriel G. Farngolo, the Superintendent of Nimba County, I understood what they meant, as his blue-blackness was different from the color of most Liberians. And I realized that, as in other countries, Liberians were very cognizant of skin tone variations.

As Peace Corp volunteers in the 1967 Liberian public administration program, our mission was to assist the various Liberian government departments in whatever ways they mandated. I was assigned to be the administrative assistant to the superintendent. I had chosen Sanniquellie, the county seat of Nimba County, because it was upcountry and at a higher altitude. I was hoping it might be a little cooler than other parts of the country.

The superintendent was very welcoming and cordial. He was an imposing man with a special aura about him who could intimidate with a stare and reassure with a smile. After graduating from the University of Liberia, he had earned a master's degree at the University of Wisconsin in education and had served as the central district supervisor of schools prior to the establishment of Nimba County in 1964.

The only problem was that the superintendent did not have any specific ideas about what to do with me. I could sense that he didn't want me involved in county politics, and now looking back, I wondered if he thought I was an American spy. After a few weeks, he took me aside and said I was being temporarily assigned to work with the relieving commission while we both thought about the best way for me to fit into his administration.

Relieving commissioner Joseph S. Miller was a jewel of a man. Kind, considerate, and funny, he often had a bemused look. In his late forties, balding and short of stature, he had plenty of experience working for the Liberian government. We took an instant liking to each other and that would prove extremely valuable in the future.

As relieving commissioner, Miller was the commissioner in waiting who would take over for a current district commissioner who might be suspended or incapacitated in some manner. One of his main duties, however, was to preside over the commissioner's court located in one of the adjacent buildings in the superintendent's compound.

Poised at his large desk and flanked by several clerks with their typewriters ready and loaded with the proper number of carbons, Miller presided over a variety of misdemeanor appellate cases mostly involving property: palavers over land use, possessions, and women. As women were considered property, these cases mainly dealt with dowries, infidelities, and paternity. All of the above could result in vociferous debates and hefty fines to correct the injustices.

While Liberian English was the official language of the court, with testimony and decisions recorded in English, most of the participants needed an interpreter. Charlie, the court interpreter, was a language genius. He knew almost all of the languages in Liberia. He also acted as the unofficial traffic cop for the court screening litigants and controlling capacity in the courtroom.

While many of the cases had a preponderance of evidence that resulted in an obvious ruling, in others, Miller skillfully managed to ferret out the pertinent information and render a decision. There were also cases where the "truth" couldn't be identified: Lying in court was a staple strategy for many of the parties concerned.

That is when the court called for the "Sassywood Man." The first time this happened, I didn't know what to think. As the court had large openings for windows, I had noticed a group of men who gathered daily and sat under one of the enormous cottonwood trees in the compound. One of the court's soldiers quickly ran to this group and summoned a man dressed in shorts and a vest. He had the composure and calmness of an experienced professional. The commissioner asked the two parties in the dispute if they were willing to undergo the "Sassywood Ritual." If one of the parties refused, then he or she was found guilty. If both agreed, the ritual would begin.

"Sassywood Man" holding court

Under the shady cottonwood tree, a cutlass was heated over a charcoal fire until red hot. The Sassywood Man said some incantations and slowly rubbed ointments from a number of pots onto the calf of the witness. He then took the hot cutlass and passed it over the exposed calf. If the calf was burned, the person was guilty. If it was not, the person was telling the truth.

I watched this ritual many times. The Sassywood Man had several ointment pots whose contents resembled the consistency of Vaseline. He spent a lot of time rubbing the defendant's leg in a solemn manner. I think that if the Sassywood Man felt trembling or a guilty reaction, he applied the ointments in one order and if he felt the opposite, he applied them in another.

In the event the calf was burned, he immediately applied a balm that soothed the burn. Once burned, you were left with a large, flat scar for life.

Sometimes, the court would intervene ahead of time to tip the balance one way or the other. I never knew when that might happen. But I had my suspicions.

Commissioner Joseph Miller was instrumental in assisting me as I developed the Nimba County Self-Help Development Program. Superintendent Farngolo was arrested as part of the Fahnbulleh "Treason" plot and dismissed from office in May 1968 on charges of embezzlement. S.T. Volker, Nimba's new Superintendent, continued to lend political support to the program.

Michael Hohl was a public administration volunteer in Sanniquellie from 1967 to 1969. He started the Nimba County Self-Help Rural Development Program. After returning to Liberia, Mike worked for Liberian-owned businesses from 1971 to 1979. He earned master's degrees in African studies and development economics from Ohio University. For the last twenty-five years, Mike has worked as a kitchen designer.

MEETING PRESIDENT TUBMAN

BY WILLIAM SWEIGART

Soon after President John F. Kennedy announced the creation of the Peace Corps, I announced, at age fifteen, I would be joining. Sure enough, six years later, after finishing my degree, I packed for Liberia to begin my service as a newly minted math and science teacher. Far from my mind was any notion that, before long, I would be under arrest for treason and sedition, standing face-to-face with President William Tubman.

The story begins in Kolahun, a rural town situated near the Sierra Leone and Guinea borders. It is far north of the capital, Monrovia, on laterite roads so rutted and washed-out during the rainy season that, at times, even the Peace Corps mail truck could not get through. In this quiet haven, I settled into a pleasant teaching routine at the junior high, a routine dramatically upset one otherwise ordinary November day.

In 1968, everyone living in Liberia understood that President William V.S. Tubman was a powerful leader. Elected president in 1944, by the 1960s, his rule did not tolerate opposition—to oppose Tubman was to oppose Liberia itself. Modeled on the U.S. system, Liberia's government had a legislative and judicial branch. However, Tubman did much of the governing himself by using "executive councils," or open sessions, which he periodically held in large town halls around the country. In these councils, Tubman acted as both president and tribal chief, adjudicating every manner of case from a neighbor's dispute over a chicken to the most serious crime. At one of these sessions, having been bizarrely charged with sedition, I met the president.

It all started on a Friday in November. I was proctoring the national exam along with other faculty. The Peace Corps mail truck arrived on Friday. Operated out of the Peace Corps office in Monrovia, the truck came once a week delivering (usually meager) teaching supplies, medications, and, of course, the mail. Because the existing Liberian postal system was not well developed, even local citizens often sent and received mail via the Peace Corps truck.

In my mail that Friday, along with several aerograms, came a white, business-sized envelope with no return information addressed to a local tribal chief, Tamba Taylor. It was late morning and proctoring had become deadly boring, so I eagerly seized the opportunity to walk into town to deliver the letter to Chief Taylor. I chatted with him as he opened the envelope and watched his growing dismay as he realized it was an anti-government tract criticizing the Tubman government. Political plutonium. Flustered, Chief Taylor immediately took the letter to the county commissioner, the highest-ranking local authority, who asked the natural question, "Where did this come from?" To which Chief Taylor replied, "The Peace Corps man brought it." Thus, accidentally and unwittingly, I had become associated with an act of treason and sedition.

The following Monday, Roosevelt Tubman, the head of the Liberian National Police Force and one of the president's sons, roared into the front yard of my Peace Corps house to arrest me. "Pack a bag," he told me, asserting that he needed to transport me to Voinjama, the county seat an hour south "for the trial." Once there, my escorts told me that I was under house arrest and should remain in the residence of the local Peace Corps volunteer. I would be on trial by the end of the week.

A trial? I could not comprehend how or why this silly misunderstanding had become so blown out of proportion. I knew enough math and science to do a decent teaching job, but I sure did not know much else. I did not have a clue what kind of danger had befallen me.

As annoying as the arrest was, I never took it seriously until the very moment the following Friday when I ended up in the executive council meeting run by President Tubman himself. In that crowded town hall, I stood in a line of people waiting to face charges. I peered around the man immediately in front of me, and there sat the president with his giant, trademark Cuban cigar. He glared at the Lebanese merchant on trial and loudly announced to an anticipating crowd, "This man is clearly guilty. Take him and lock him up without bail." At that moment, terrified, I worried I might pass out. As guards led the hapless shopkeeper off and ushered me toward the president, somebody read a description of the seditious materials that had somehow reached the hands of Chief Tamba Taylor. Tubman glanced up at me and said, "Tell us what happened."

I remember almost nothing from that moment forward except the overwhelming feeling of trepidation and nervousness. Obviously, I spoke, and apparently very convincingly, because the next thing I do remember was Tubman saying, "It's clear this Peace Corps man had nothing to do with this crime, and he needs to be released." I thought I heard murmurs of approval from the audience, but I was unsure.

What happened next seemed just as astonishing as everything that had come before. While being ushered from the pavilion, students and teachers from my school in Kolahun surrounded me, shook my hand, and congratulated me on my release. I still felt flummoxed at how the simple act of delivering a letter to Chief Taylor had led to this bizarre, dramatic turn. I was highly relieved and happy that day to return to Kolahun and my ninth-grade algebra class.

The Peace Corps administration from Monrovia did not communicate with me before, during, or after the trial. Only much later did I learn that they had been at the ready with a small plane on the flight strip in Voinjama. The staff had my passport on board in advance to spirit me out of Liberia if things had gone badly with the president.

Within a week, I was "Teacher Bill," back in the classroom with my students practicing algebra. To the best of my recollection, we never spoke of the event again. Happily, I completed the final years of my teaching assignment pretty much without incident.

William Sweigart began a forty-six-year teaching career in Liberia (1967 to 1970), where he taught math and science in junior high, along with first grade. Subsequently, he taught university-level English, including at the teacher-training program at Stanford. Having retired from Indiana University Southeast in 2014, he now spends as much time as possible in Costa Rica, where he tries to learn Spanish.

PASSING THE TEST

BY JOE JAUREGUI

I arrived in Liberia, West Africa, in 1967, one of a large contingent of Peace Corps volunteer teachers who, at the government's request, were assigned to schools throughout the country. The classrooms included a significant number of students from poor families.

One formidable obstacle for students was passing the Liberian national exam. This exam was given to students who completed the sixth, ninth, and twelfth grades. In order to be promoted to the next grade or graduate, a student needed to pass the exam. Many students who failed the exam were not given a second chance to stay in school and take the exam again. For the impoverished students, failure on the test could mean they would return to their village and their path toward opportunity would become more challenging.

I realized how important education was for my students when I learned that a majority of the fifty-five fifth- and sixth-graders lived in the outlying countryside. They came to stay with extended families in Gbarnga to attend one of several public or mission schools in town. Since education was not free, the students would work to pay for their school fees, room, and board. As long as a student succeeded in school, that student was able to stay on the road to future achievements.

Fresh out of college, I was determined to teach my students how to reason for themselves and be able to learn enough about the world to enable them to make informed decisions. This lasted about two weeks.

The need to pass the national exam, and the years they were taught to learn by rote, dictated that I coach my students for the examination. I shifted my determination to focus on preparing my students to pass the examination so they could continue their quest for a better life.

There were no textbooks. The students only felt comfortable when I was writing on the pockmarked chalkboard so they could copy the lesson in their notebooks to later memorize. The national exam was published in Boston. Not only did I have to teach test-taking strategies, I had to describe what a train was before they could understand how long it would take that train leaving New York City going fifty miles per hour to reach Boston. Snow was another concept. There were no trains or snow in the equatorial rain forest of upcountry Liberia. Eventually, I was able to obtain some study guides and get an idea of what the exam encompassed. I was able to use the mimeograph machine in the Peace Corps office in town. The hand-cranked machine proved to be a godsend.

Joe serving meals to the students, 1968

The students were very diligent. Occasionally, some missed school because they had to work on the family farm. There were never issues with discipline. The students' desire to pass the exam made them ever-attentive. Some days, though, the equatorial sun was unrelenting and the humidity was almost as high as the temperature. My clothes were soaking wet. On these days, the students were restless and didn't care how long it took a train to get from Boston to Los Angeles. To get their attention, I would pick up a piece of chalk and walk to the board and start writing. After a short while, I could hear the rustle of students reaching for their notebooks, then silence, as they started to copy what I was writing.

I didn't learn the fate of my students on the exam until after I returned home to the United States. A letter from the principal informed me that fifty-two of the fifty-five students I taught passed the exam. He said it was one of the highest passing rates in the country. I wish I could have seen the students' reactions when they learned of their results, and tell them how proud I was of their accomplishments. They studied. They put the work in. And, when it was all said and done, they ended that academic year with an incredible achievement, and I was left with one of the greatest experiences an educator can have.

Joe Jauregui was a Peace Corps volunteer in Gbarnga, Liberia, from 1967 to 1969. He taught at St. Martin's Catholic Mission. Afterward, he continued his career as an educator, serving as a teacher and administrator in Ventura County, California, for thirty-five years. He and his wife of forty-nine years raised a family and have been active as volunteers in community organizations.

RECURRING LIFE LESSON

BY ELIZABETH FLEMING FROST

"Thank you" was my only response when a young Liberian boy offered to sit on his mother's lap so that I could have the seat by the window. I squeezed in beside the family. A man appeared from nowhere and slammed the rear money-taxi door.

Adventure was at the forefront of my thinking. In 1969, I exchanged a world of graduate school and Washington, D.C., debutante parties for a country on the West Coast of Africa. Tired of how I was supposed to carry myself in society, according to certain handed-down rules and traditions, I was ready for the Livingstone experience.

Chatter began in broken English, asking where I was from, what does Hollywood really look like, how long on the plane to get from the U.S. to Liberia, etc. I politely answered all of the questions, but the question-chatter continued. The red dust swirled up my nose and into my eyes. By the time the money-taxi driver stepped on the gas, my eyes were closed and a bandana covered my nose. Needless to say, what a surprise when the driver braked suddenly, forcing my body forward. He yelled, "Compound One, Peace Corps stop!"

Compound One was a unique village. It was made up of people from various ethnic groups, settled there by the Liberian government after the closing of the Firestone Rubber Plantation (when synthetic rubber became available) and after the transfer of the Monrovia airport from U.S. to

Liberian control. Many Liberians who had worked for Firestone and for U.S. personnel at the airport lost their jobs and became displaced persons.

I opened my eyes to a scene from an old Western movie. Instead of horses and cowboy hats, there was a man dressed in a coat and tails, rocking on the front porch of the wooden general store. As the dust settled, excited school-aged children gathered around the taxi, all eager to help carry my gear. Once the money-taxi fare was paid, and the driver realized there was not another fare on to Buchanan, he left as fast as the gas pedal allowed.

The man in the coat and tails turned out to be Mr. Lee, the official Americo-Liberian town representative designated to welcome me to the village. He also was the owner of the Peace Corps house. He and his wife proudly walked down the porch steps to greet their bewildered guest. My stereotypical expectation of jungle scenery, people wearing plant or animal-made clothing, tall spears, and mud and thatch-roofed homes in a circle was shattered. My three-month Peace Corps training had taken place in Monrovia, the capital of Liberia, and a relatively cosmopolitan city. Monrovia was my "visual" to Liberia. My expectations were shaped, as well, by the many current *New York Times*' articles featuring the African nations gaining freedom from English colonization.

I looked to the right and saw a fellow Peace Corps volunteer. Thank goodness for another teacher who would live along with me in Compound One. David spoke quietly and directed me toward his home. We were followed by a line of school children sharing my gear. I had never experienced being the total center of attention. Once in the living quarters of David's house, the gear was piled into the front room, which was also the school. I was offered a wet washcloth, a glass of water, and a glass of sherry.

The following days were spent being introduced to village elders by Mr. Lee. On Friday, the small parade of Compound One elders made their way to the chief's home. As the wooden door opened, I was engulfed by color: front covers of *Better Homes and Gardens'* magazines were used as colorful wallpaper to enhance the room's décor. The chief's wife wore a brightly colored headdress and matching *lappa* and blouse with extremely puffy sleeves. The colors were as bright as the magazine covers. Wooden chairs, obviously recently purchased in a Monrovia store, were placed in a circle. Each chair still had the sales tag attached. I believed that the chief was displaying the wealth of the community. Each elder knew his assigned seat. I was given the seat to the left of the chief. The chief's wife sat to his right. The chief introduced me to the Compound One elders as "the new white doctor for the clinic." I was stunned.

My Peace Corps placement was based, I assumed, on the experience and skills I had described in my application. I had volunteered in hospitals and residential settings for crippled children and had set up an after-school program for special needs children. My BA thesis focused on the importance of nutrition and learning. By no means was my three months of community health training in Liberia an MD degree!

I sat in disbelief. My ability to respond was hampered by a dry frog taking up residence in my throat. After only five days in this unique village, I was still clueless as to its cultural ways. I knew, only too well, that if I didn't meet the group's expectations, it could ultimately threaten my Peace Corps mission to develop a pre- and post-natal baby clinic and gain the confidence of the community and the midwives. I also knew I wanted to be judged on my own merits and not on preconceived ideas from other people or from predetermined cultural assumptions, the same situation I had escaped from in the U.S. Once again, I faced expectations that made me feel I had to run away.

At that moment, as I sat in the circle of community leaders, I realized running from a problem did not solve it.

The salty sweat covering my body stung my eyes and brought me back to the circle. I had the floor to speak with purpose. During my presentation, I did my best to clarify the Peace Corps health care plan and to straighten out the misunderstanding of my credentials. By the time I had finished my presentation, this community of villagers and the Americo-Liberians were on board.

My lesson of life had come full circle.

Elizabeth Fleming Frost was part of Group 17 Peace Corps Volunteer Compound One in Grand Bassa County, from 1969 to 1970. She was a health educator who acquired a master's degree in speech and language pathology and worked in the medical field, private practice, and public schools. Retired, she continues to work with incarcerated adolescents and to travel the world.

GREETINGS

BY DOROTHY WRASE HARES

In 1971, after two weeks of in-country Peace Corps training in Liberia, I entered the John F. Kennedy Medical Center in the capital of Monrovia and said "Hi" to the woman at the information desk. She blinked her eyes, indicating to me an affirmation, so I continued. "I'll be working in the kitchen, but this is my first time here. Could you direct me to the kitchen?"

She waited a moment, and then slowly said, "Good Morning!" I remembered from my training that until proper greetings were completed, the next phase of conversation with a person could not continue.

"Good Morning!" I said, and smiled.

She nodded her head and asked, "How may I help you?"

After I located the kitchen, I met with the Liberian dietitian to begin my in-hospital training. When I told her that I was embarrassed about not remembering the importance of starting with "Good Morning," she proposed an idea. "There are people working here from many different tribes. Let's have you learn the greetings of several of them."

That day I learned the greeting in Bassa, the language used by the kitchen workers. I also learned that the greeting and the response could vary depending on the time of day. A few days later, I learned the Vai greeting in order to say hello to workers in the nearby laundry unit. In each of the various departments of the hospital—such as housekeeping, maintenance, and central supply—only people from a single ethnic group worked there, so I had many opportunities to practice the greetings of many languages. Each ethnic group had its own distinct language. It was not just an accent or a matter of a few words of dialect.

After a few weeks, I began working on the patient units. I carefully noted the patient's ethnic group and said their greeting. They often responded with surprise, but then began speaking only in their language and pointing to specific areas of their body. From a simple greeting, they assumed I knew their language.

Eventually, I was given office space on the top floor of the hospital. The top floor was where patients who were important elected officials or political appointees were located. Although bigwigs were not frequently hospitalized, it did mean that I had to pass through a security check to reach my office.

One day, when a VIP was admitted as an inpatient, my work schedule unfortunately meant being in and out of my office more than usual. By late afternoon, I was going through the security process for the seventh time that day. I continued to use Liberian English and was pleasant to the same two security people I'd passed for the previous six reviews. When they had completed their work and nodded that I could proceed, I asked, "Don't I look at least familiar to you since I have done this with you a number of times today?"

They looked at each other and then one of them said, "Well, all you white people look the same."

Sometimes I would take one of the elevators to go to the top floor office. I noticed that when people entered the elevator they would say, "Good Morning to All!" Saying these words became part of my boarding-the-elevator routine.

Several years later, this ingrained habit became part of my automatic greeting when I resumed work in a U.S. hospital. I entered the elevator one early morning and said, "Good Morning to All!" The group of people in the Duluth hospital looked very puzzled.

Then, the person standing by the control panel said, "Okay, you are on your way to the fifth floor."

I then realized they thought I was going to (and perhaps belonged on) the "Psych" unit. As I walked off the elevator, the words *beta beta nu bek bek* popped into my mind—Bassa for "take your time, slow down."

In 2014, the Ebola pandemic was devastating Liberia. The Obama Administration recognized that Ebola could impact health care in the U.S., and encouraged hospitals in New York to develop a plan. I worked alongside several Liberians in a Syracuse hospital, and a group of us approached one of the administrators, whose brother was a returned Peace Corps volunteer. We offered to help by sharing cultural information. A few days later, while visiting with Suzanne, a cashier who grew up in Liberia, the nursing leader for the Ebola project approached us to ask for our help. "Could you provide me with a few Liberian greetings so that when someone from Liberia is admitted to St. Joseph's Hospital, we could make them feel more comfortable by greeting them in their language?"

Suzanne and I looked at each other. She greeted me in Gio, and I gave the response. Then I greeted her in Bassa and she responded. We noted that those were the greetings of only two of the tribes and we began to think out loud together. I could do Vai. She could do Kpelle.

The nursing leader asked, "Wait a minute, there are more than two-to-three tribes in Liberia?"

We laughed, "Yes, there are sixteen tribes."

The nursing leader responded, "Oh this might be more complicated. Let me get back to you."

Our response was Liberian—a quick inhaled expression of "*huhh*" meaning "okay."

To greet a person by using their language is a marvelous way to begin a human interaction. Learning the greetings allowed me to feel at home in Liberia; however, one should always be prepared for complications and misunderstandings. "*Beta beta nu bek bek!*"

Dorothy Wrase Hares served as a Peace Corps nutrition volunteer at John F. Kennedy Medical Center in Monrovia from 1971 to 1973. In the U.S., she obtained a master's degree and became a registered dietitian/nutritionist. She met and married Bill, RPCV Liberia, 1972 to 1974. Their lives of raising a son, advocating for democracy and peace, and traveling continue to be a great adventure.

ONE PERSON AT A TIME

BY SUSAN E. GREISEN

Amand walked through our clinic door cradling his six-year-old son Saye. The boy was emaciated and unable to walk. A tattered, dirty T-shirt and shorts hung on his shoeless, stick-like body. The father heard rumors of the "white-woman doctor" in Zorgowee and carried Saye over three miles in his last desperate effort to save his critically ill son.

It was 1973 and I was in my second year as a Peace Corps health education volunteer. I was the first health volunteer assigned to this rural clinic built two years earlier in the small village of Zorgowee, with just a thousand people. The clinic had no trained midwives or doctors, just an assistant with first-aid-type training. Only a few larger surrounding towns had traditional Western medicine practices brought to the region by missionaries a couple of decades earlier. Through my teachings, the villagers had begun to see some improvements in their health, such as better nutrition and more effective treatment of minor illnesses. Over time, my reputation as a healer or adjunct to their traditional country medicine gradually took hold. However, at age twenty, with only a practical nursing certificate, I was far from being a "doctor."

I concluded that Saye suffered from severe kwashiorkor, a state of protein malnutrition. Previously, I had only read about this ailment in medical textbooks. He presented with the classic symptoms: a bloated abdomen, puffy face, swollen feet and hands, spindly arms and legs, and brittle blond hair. Listless, without a trace of a smile, he had lost one-quarter to one-third of his normal body weight.

I learned that Saye had experienced severe diarrhea months prior, and his family chose to treat this condition with country herbs and potions through the local medicine man. These treatments may have resolved his diarrhea before he was brought to our clinic. However, the medicine man informed Amand that Saye was witched. And, to rid him of the curse, he needed additional herbs and rituals for him to regain weight. Amand followed this guidance along with a prescribed diet of white rice with no protein. After weeks of this regimen, the medicine man's treatment ultimately led to the boy's kwashiorkor. I soon learned that country medicine practices were hard to influence even when those methods were ineffective. Many locals still believed in them.

Traditionally, the hierarchy of food distribution meant that children received the least protein, an inadequate amount of about a teaspoon for an entire day. With protein as the most expensive food and harder to acquire, it was customary that men received the most protein, followed by women and children last. In addition, an ill child often received no traditional protein, such as meat, which is hard to digest. White rice filled the child's stomach but lacked sufficient nutrition.

Peter, our clinic health assistant, and I worked to help Amand and his malnourished boy. I explained about the importance of providing protein-rich foods. Peter translated my instructions into Gio. Our clinic was stocked with only first-aid-type supplies; therefore, we placed our main hope in the vegetable oil and powdered milk supplied by CARE. I demonstrated how to make a nutritious rice cereal with these food supplements that provided the necessary fat and protein and would be easily tolerated.

Over several weeks, Saye became stronger as he resumed a normal diet. His bloated belly, puffy face, swollen feet and hands shrunk, and muscle mass returned. The blond brittle hair gradually disappeared and was replaced by a jet-black growth. Slowly, but surely, the six-year-old became strong enough to walk, something he hadn't done in months. After weeks of care and monitoring, I experienced my first joy: I caught Saye's smile.

Four months had passed when Amand and his son stood at my front door.

"*Ba bua*, Younga Ti."

"*Aa-oo*," I replied.

I gestured for them to come in. The father spoke softly in the few Liberian English words he knew, "Younga Ti, my two wives and five children say thank you, ya, for saving Saye. We want to give you Saye for yur own." He paused, took a deep breath, and went on, "You can take good, good care of Saye, mo' better than me. Take, Saye, I beg you, ya."

I paused, searching for words . . . any words. I inhaled deeply then responded in my best Liberian English, "Amand, I thank you and yur family for all good you do for Saye and bring him to clinic. I am so happy for his good, good health."

"Yes. You save him," Amand pleaded.

I swallowed the lump rising in my throat and replied, "Amand, thank you, ya, for yur kindness. But . . . Saye need his family. Saye need his village and his people. Saye need you, his father. I could never give dat to him. I would take him back to America where all would be so so different. You can give Saye his family, his village, and his people. You did a good job. You are a good, good father."

Amand's eyes fell and his shoulders slumped. I was uncertain if it indicated disappointment or relief. Displaying the traditional Liberian gesture of respect, I bowed my head and grasped my right forearm with my left as I shook Amand's hand. He bowed in return.

Then my chest swelled when my eyes met Saye's longing gaze. Did he know we were talking about him, as he understood no English? My knees nearly buckled as I bent down and gave him the biggest hug. I dared not blink to contain my tears.

"Younga Ti, thank you, ya. Thank you, thank you." Amand choked on his words. "You are a good, good white-woman doctor. I now take Saye back to my family." The grateful father took his son's hand, and just as they approached my front door, both turned to me and smiled, then departed.

I believed Amand was a caring father. He sought the resources with which he was familiar. He offered me the only valued thing he had to give for saving his first-born—the most precious of the Liberian children—and that was to give me his son.

When I awoke the following morning, I was glad to have helped Saye return to health. And I remembered the lesson I'd learned over my two years: I couldn't save everyone. The most I could hope to accomplish was to help one person, one family at a time.

Susan E. Greisen served in Peace Corps Liberia from 1971 to 1973, and Tonga, from 1973 to 1974, as a health education volunteer. She later worked as an RN public health specialist for CARE in Cameroon from 1980 to 1982. Susan was honored to lead the FOL project that published this anthology. Her award-winning memoir, *In Search of Pink Flamingos*, features her time in Liberia. Learn more at susangreisen.com.

INTO THE RAIN FOREST

BY JANA BERTKAU

The single engine plane is just big enough for three people and some luggage. We sit at the end of the small Monrovia city runway ready to take off for eastern Liberia, the area inhabited by speakers of the Kru language. This is my first foray away from the teeming city of Monrovia. The missionary pilot bows his head and prays: "Lord, guide us today and allow us to complete our journey as we seek to do your work. Amen." I worry that divine help may be needed as I sweat in the oppressive humidity.

The other passenger is John Duitsman, a missionary linguist and my unlikely partner in a research project to survey the dialects of the Kru language. It is 1974, I am twenty-four, and a newly minted Ph.D. in linguistics. My Peace Corps job description: "Analyze the languages of Liberia (there are about twenty), reduce them to writing (I specialize in language learning, not African languages), create curriculum to teach the native children to read and write their own languages." I have no idea how to manage this but am idealistic and ready to make a difference in the world.

I had stumbled upon John shortly upon arrival in Liberia. He was one of the Lutheran Bible translators with The Institute for Liberian Languages. The Institute's mission was basically the same as mine. I quickly realized these people knew what they were doing. My Liberian boss at the Ministry of Education, Mrs. Azango, allowed me to partner with the missionaries, and, while I questioned their proselytizing, I respected their linguistic knowledge.

We fly above thick green rain forest with no sign of roads, villages, or people. I wonder how many lost planes are buried in this expanse. But that only makes me hotter and sweatier. *Stop thinking like that, Jana. Focus on the upcoming task.*

Our overall assignment is to record a list of two hundred words from thirty-eight villages to determine how wide the Kru language is spread. This is our first trip, and I worry about how we will conduct this assignment, and how the pilot will find the village in this expanse of jungle. At last, a village and adjacent runway appear, and we trundle to a stop.

The next morning, we are assigned a young man to guide us into the rain forest to a village for our research. We traipse down the beach. The sun blazes and the humidity drags on me. We cross a small estuary in a canoe-like boat and enter on foot into the rain forest. The path winds deeper and deeper into the green. The trees rise thickly around us, cutting out the sun. Insects buzz, monkeys chatter. The humidity does not abate. My homemade country cloth dress clings to my body. What is lurking in the gloom? The guide is unperturbed; I calm down and trudge on. Then, we stop cold. An army of driver ants is marching across the path. I have been in Liberia long enough to know that driver ants are what people fear more than snakes. Driver ants are known to surround a hut and quickly clean out anything edible. You don't want them to decide that you are a tasty treat.

The guide says, "Don't worry, ya. They na hungry now. Just run quick, quick." This excitement is repeated several times.

After a few hours, we reach the outskirts of a village. A few small boys see us approaching and run away in fear. I wonder if these boys have ever seen a white person. I feel my white skin glow in the dark forest.

John, who is a pro at village visits, has stashed some tobacco in his shirt pocket, making sure it is visible. "You will see how interested the village elders will become when they see the tobacco."

Sure enough, we are welcomed. John distributes his tobacco, and our guide explains the purpose of the visit. With great excitement, a table is set up in the shade of a tree. Our tape recorder is brought out and we begin our work. Every child in the village gathers around to gawk, giggle, and wonder. When we finish, a village chicken is caught and prepared for a special dinner in our honor.

The next morning, we retrace our steps through the forest, the driver ants, and the estuary, and return to the coastal village.

"Is the pilot coming back to get us?" I ask.

"No," John says, "he was not available. No problem! We can catch the coastal shuttle plane."

"What time is that flight due?" I ask.

"Oh, sometime in the morning. You have to flag the pilot by waving something white."

I am flabbergasted.

At the grass field we peer at the sky. Eventually, we hear the sound of a plane and frantically wave our white shirts. I am extremely relieved when the plane turns and lands. It is small, with six seats, all of which are occupied.

"No problem," says the Spanish pilot, and chickens and goats are shifted to make room.

Jana on her linguistics assignment

The heavy plane bounces down the grass runway, very slowly gaining speed. In front, the jungle grows larger, and I worry that we will not lift in time to clear the thick trees. The Liberian woman sitting next to me grabs my leg. I smile at her trying to calm my own nerves. Finally, we skim above the trees and head over the ocean. I breathe a bit easier and gaze at the choppy waves and sandy beach. I will be home soon.

My universe has shifted. I have moved from a land of order and predictability to an unimagined land of adventure, surprises, and unlikely friendships; from being the white majority to being the white minority.

Did I make a difference in Liberia? I don't know. My stamp on Liberia was probably small. My research did result in one published paper co-authored with two missionary linguists, some unpublished papers, and a Bassa reading primer, which I introduced in a Bassa-speaking school. I am proud of these results, but these tangible outcomes pale in comparison to the benefits I received from my experience. After forty-eight years, a sense of astonishment lingers with me still. Those two Peace Corps years comprised an intense period of complete cultural transplantation with a steep learning curve and significant personal growth. I am hugely proud of this period of my life and recognize that I brought out of it a recognition of the diversity in our world, the advantages I was born into, and gratitude for the experience.

Jana Bertkau was a Peace Corps volunteer in Monrovia from 1973 to 1975, and worked for the Ministry of Education as a linguist. She conducted language surveys, language analyses, and developed Bassa primers. Jana and her husband, Richard (PCV lawyer 1973-1975), are retired on Martha's Vineyard and enjoy traveling, hiking, gardening, skiing, volunteering, and visiting three children and six grandchildren.

UNCOMMON MEAT

BY ELOISE ANNETTE CAMPBELL

As the wooden boat weaved through the clumps of latex in the raunchy Farmington River late that Friday, I reviewed my grocery list to make sure I remembered to add sweetened condensed milk for OD, my Liberian grandmother, who couldn't get enough of the stuff. Most importantly, I needed to make sure that I picked up dog food for Toga, the dog of my fellow PC friend Bruce. Toga meant "man of war" in Bassa and the name fit him perfectly—strong, brave, and fit. Bruce added a raw egg and some palm oil to the dog food. Toga's coat was shiny and healthy-looking and the envy of every mangy, scrawny mutt in Fortsville.

It was May 1974. I had been a Peace Corps teacher in Liberia for only six months. Going to market was a daily task. The boat trip from Owensgrove to Harbel was just ten minutes, but the stench from the latex factory made the trip seem to last twice as long. As I disembarked, I secured my wallet around my neck, grabbed my list and a flashlight, and headed on the short trip to the store. I took the flashlight, anticipating a night of partying that might go into the early hours. The last time I had tried to use my night vision without the aid of the flashlight, I had kicked something that turned out to be a giant scorpion. You never knew what was lurking in the dark. I didn't want to chance my luck a second time.

I made my way down the path through the brush until I arrived at the store. It was always a happy place, with highlife music blaring and dancing already underway. Sami and Fayad's Lebanese store was not only a place to get grocery items and dry goods, it was a popular place to unwind with the locals over a bottle of Club Beer. Sami and Fayad were brothers, and both had a delightful sense of humor. On a Friday evening, locals, Peace Corps volunteers, and Liberian and American employees from the Firestone Rubber Plantation would congregate there. Today was no different.

Amstel was Sami and Fayad's loyal, enormous, German Shepherd dog they had brought from Beirut. Feared by all Liberians and Americans alike at Firestone, Amstel was the perfect guard dog. He was impressive in size and was the best fed dog in all of Harbel, maybe all of Liberia. Toga was a close second.

Women danced gracefully in their *lappas*. I was always impressed that the wrapped cloth skirts didn't slip down. Seeing everyone having such a wonderful time distracted me from the task at hand, but I didn't mind. This was what I enjoyed most about my experience in Africa. That night we all danced and laughed as we let the stresses of the week slip away, oblivious to the terror lurking nearby. Time passed by quickly, and before long, it was closing time. The store generator was shut down, but the party continued at Sami and Fayad's attached apartment. The kerosene lamps were lit, and the music played on. The fun continued.

Suddenly, the excruciating yelping of a dog sounded above the music. Without hesitation, Sami grabbed his gun from the rack on the wall while Fayad got in the car to shine the headlights toward the sound of howling. I was afraid to look and not sure what was happening, so I stayed behind Sami. The howling was very disturbing, as there was no doubt that it was Amstel in a lot of pain. Fahad finally got the headlights directed at Amstel. I was prepared to witness someone breaking into the store and maybe taking a machete to Amstel. All that was visible was an enormous python coiled around the dog. The only part of Amstel that was visible was his hind leg. A skilled marksman, Sami waited for the snake to elevate its head and when it did, he got a clear shot. All at once, gigantic snake coils unraveled in an incredibly grotesque fashion. Sami rushed over with several others to pull the enormous python off Amstel, who by this time had ceased howling. There was silence. Everyone was in shock. None of us had ever seen such a gigantic python, let alone witnessed one torturing a beloved pet. Sami encouraged everyone to assist in pulling the snake off the dog. It was awkward to pull away heavy armfuls of this monster, whose muscles still seemed to be moving and writhing. Despite our efforts to revive Amstel, sadly, he was dead.

We tried comforting Sami and Fayad, but it did little to ease their suffering. Some of the Liberians started digging a grave for Amstel behind the store, while others, under the direction of Fayad, skinned and cut the twenty-foot-long, one hundred thirty-five-pound python into one-foot sections. The Liberian workers at the store carried the snake meat to market but quickly returned with it. The villagers had said it was taboo to eat snake in their village. The workers went to bury the snake, only to discover that Amstel's grave was dug up and the body removed. Snake meat might not have been on the menu, but a well-fed German Shepherd evidently was.

I wasn't prepared for villagers to eat the meat of a pet animal. But when Toga died the following year, he was also dug up. As I wrestled with my feelings, I came to understand that in a region where valuable protein was hard to find, it was not uncommon to eat dog. I came to accept that my American sentiments about dogs did not belong in Liberia. Liberians had learned how to survive, and I had learned to challenge my preconceived beliefs.

After Eloise Annette Campbell taught math and sciences in Ganta and Owensgrove, Liberia, in Group 41, from 1973 to 1975, she traveled extensively through West Africa, Kenya, Tanzania, and Egypt. She returned to Ohio and received her Juris Doctorate degree and represented indigents through Legal Aid and neglected children as a court appointed special advocate. Along with her family, Eloise enjoys sailing and boating on Lake Erie.

SEVEN-AND-A-HALF CHAIRS

BY SALLY SALISBURY ZELONIS

In 1971, after six weeks of in-country Peace Corps training at the luxurious Voice of America compound in Monrovia, I was sent to the Gio village of Karnplay, far from the capital, for a week of instruction in the local language. Gio is a very guttural language and was nothing like other languages I had studied before. There were no books and no written alphabet. My teacher was also an instructor at Karnplay Elementary, where I would be teaching. We met every day for five days. How do you learn a language in five days? I could barely give the standard greeting, "*Babua*," let alone the response, "*aa-oo*." I did try, but my tongue and throat really didn't seem to cooperate.

My first day of school arrived. Fresh out of college, with just a semester of teaching experience, I was understandably nervous. My plan was to go to school, enter my classroom, take attendance, get a feel for what I was facing, and then call it a day. Seemed like a good plan to me. After all, I only had five days of language training and I had no idea if my students could speak English! So much unknown.

I climbed the hill to school with my rice bag satchel, a notebook, pencil, and some chalk. I stood with the Liberian teachers at the flag ceremony and was introduced by the principal. When I looked out in front of me, there were six long rows of students numbering at least several hundred!

The teachers were dismissed to their classrooms. I walked to mine and found a table, a cabinet, two chalkboards, and seven-and-a-half chairs.

How do you get half of a chair? You cut it right down the middle! How would this accommodate the throngs of students who stood outside? This was nothing like my teacher training in Monrovia, where we had plenty of books and plenty of furniture.

In came ninety students. They rushed in like a blur as I stood at the front of the classroom. It was a mad rush—no pushing, just moving fast, clamoring to grab the chairs and floor space wherever they could find it. When the dust and noise settled, at least two students were sitting on every chair, and the "half" chair had two students trying to balance between wobbles. Every corner of the room was occupied.

I was so glad I had decided to just take attendance and then call it a day. We had done some Teaching English as a Second Language (TESL) training while in Monrovia. This was helpful but only to a point. I talked for about ten minutes, using hand gestures and asking students to repeat after me. An ocean of eyes focused on me. I then told them that they were dismissed for the day. I must have said it ten times, re-phrasing it each time: "You are dismissed now. You can go home now. I will see you tomorrow. Thank you for coming." Finally, a young boy in the front row jumped up, turned around, and shouted something in Gio. Ninety students ran out of the classroom. His name was Johnny Glee—he became my prized second-grade student.

My students faced many challenges in getting to school every day. Many had no food, no uniforms, a long distance to walk, chores on the farm—these were just some of the obstacles they faced. I learned early on that if I did not lock my door to the classroom after the bell rang, students would walk in all day. Once I figured this out, students late to class would go to the slatted windows and hang on them to listen to the lesson—passing their homework to a willing classmate to hand in. I marveled at their eagerness to learn that superseded any difficulties they faced.

Upon returning back to the U.S., I began teaching a first-grade class in New Hampshire. In all my years of teaching in the United States, I never had a class as large as Karnplay, never had a class without materials, never had a class with half a chair, never had a class where eighty percent of the students stood or sat on the floor, and never had a class of students so eager to learn, no matter the odds.

I carry my Liberian lessons of life and learning, including the seven-and-a-half chairs, with me to this very day—fifty years later.

Sally (Salisbury) Zelonis taught elementary school as a Peace Corps volunteer in Karnplay, Liberia, from 1971 to 1972. Upon returning home, she married her husband, Mark, also a Peace Corps volunteer. After several years teaching, Sally began a twenty-five-year career in fundraising for nonprofits. Sally and her husband live in Zionsville, Indiana. She serves on the board of directors for Friends of Liberia.

A DAY IN THE CLINIC

BY SUSAN CORBETT

On a blue morning of sailing clouds, I crossed the clearing that separated my house from the two-room clinic, which was the only health facility within a twenty-mile radius of thick bush and rain forest. A breeze carried the voices of chatting mothers and crying babies. Today was Under Five's Day—the weekly clinic for babies and children up to five years old. In 1978, well into my second year as a Peace Corps volunteer in the tiny bush town of Foequelleh, I worked at the clinic giving nutrition demonstrations and vaccinating children.

Awake from my morning cup of Nescafé and ready for the day, I passed through the dappled shade of a cottonwood tree. It was the town's Ancestor Tree, where the ghosts of great-great-grandfathers, great-aunts, uncles, and cousins hid in the hollows of the trunk with snakes and spiders and high up in the branches among the leaves and ricebirds. The Ancestor Tree loomed next to a red dirt road that twisted its way around the clinic, past my house at the end of town, and on through lush hillside plots of rice, potato greens, and cassava.

Women with babies tied to their backs in cloth slings gathered at the clinic door. They entered and stacked their yellow "Road to Health" cards in a pile that reserved their place. Then, they sat on benches to wait their turn and catch up on local gossip.

James, the clinic janitor and local translator, joined me in the waiting room, a twenty-by-ten-foot space with a dirt floor and mud-plastered walls that smelled of baby pee and sweat. We said our good mornings. I stood in the center and began to squeeze oranges into a bowl. Side by side, James and I explained the causes and treatment of diarrhea, me in Liberian English and James in Kpelle, the local language. As I demonstrated the pinch of salt and teaspoon of sugar needed to make rehydration fluid, a woman came in with a round-faced little girl in tattered shorts and cornrow braids. The pair sat at the end of the bench, and the little girl lay her head on her mother's shoulder and closed her eyes.

Over the next few hours, James and I worked with Francis, the local physician's assistant. We weighed babies, treated skin and stomach ailments, distributed malaria medication, and vaccinated against smallpox, whooping cough, and tetanus. Morning cool gave way to the heat of the day, and the rooms grew stuffy. Sometime before noon, I walked back into the waiting room to call the next in line.

The woman with the little girl took her daughter's hand and led her into the room. The girl, about five years old, tried to stand but collapsed. Her mother caught her, and I ran to grasp the girl's arm. Her skin burned, and her lips were chapped and dry. She breathed out a rattled sigh, and her head lolled to one side.

"Francis! James!" I called.

They came in an instant.

James laid the little girl down, her skinny arms and legs limp against the floor. Francis bent his ear to her nose, then felt her wrist for a pulse. He looked up at us and shook his head. Her mother began to wail.

I knelt, unable to believe, unable to understand. In my two years at the clinic, this had never happened. I had never seen a person die. The spark of the little girl who had been with us only a moment before was gone. Without thought, I propped her head back, pressed my mouth over hers, and blew my breath into her limp, dehydrated body. Her skinny chest lifted then deflated. Francis pumped her chest, and I blew into her lungs again, then again.

There was no ambulance to call, no emergency room to whisk her to. The clinic was the only place. We tried for a while longer until Francis put his hand on my arm. "She is gone," he said.

Her black irises were dull, as if a door at the back of her eyes had shut, blocking out the light. Yet, her skin was warm and smelled the way children smell, an earthy sweetness that no amount of dirt can hide. Francis gently pressed her eyelids closed. The bleat of a baby goat echoed across the clearing.

Amidst the mother's wails and the silent grief of the other women, the muscles of my throat closed into a fist. The woman had brought in her child, sick with dysentery, dehydrated, dying, and she had sat and waited her turn.

Why had I not noticed when they first came in? Why had I not done something sooner? I looked around at the faces of the women and children who still crowded the room and I started to cry. The mothers all turned to me, eyebrows raised, mouths open, as if they realized for the first time that I, too, was made of flesh and bone.

A week later, several of my students put on a skit at a school gathering. A young man lay on the ground while another pantomimed blowing air into his mouth. Everyone laughed, inviting me to share in the jest.

Foolish Miss Soosan, thinking that by blowing, she could chase away death.

My flushed cheeks and blank face must have moved them. They patted me on the back and spoke kind words, the way one treats someone who simply doesn't know any better.

Foolish Miss Soosan, crying because she could not make someone stay when they had already left.

Susan Corbett worked as a Peace Corps health volunteer in Foequelleh, Liberia, Bong County, from 1976 to 1979. She earned a master's degree in nonprofit management and worked for Save the Children in Burkina Faso from 1980 to 1982. Susan is the author of *In the Belly of the Elephant*, a memoir of Africa, and currently teaches ESL to immigrant adults. She lives in Colorado.

A LASSA FEVER JOURNEY

BY JUDY MARCOUILLER

I guess the fact that I'd survived a rare hemorrhagic fever virus didn't sink in until after I was discharged from the hospital and regained my strength in a Monrovia guesthouse in January 1979. I overheard the guesthouse owner talking on the phone about a "contagious" Peace Corps volunteer. Later that day, a Peace Corps staffer came by to pick me up and transfer me to a Peace Corps staff house while the Peace Corps and various medical experts decided what should be done with me.

My journey began in December 1978, when I was coordinating graduation meal preparations at Zorzor Rural Teacher Training Institute (ZTI) in Lofa County, where I served as one of two home economics teacher trainers. The home economics department was traditionally expected to prepare a meal for several hundred following the graduation ceremony. My Liberian counterpart led the second-year "home ec" students as they prepared the main meal components of rice and various savory sauces. I was expected to lead the first-year students in preparation of westernized (or "*kwi*") accompaniments: fruit drinks, cakes, and other desserts.

The baking ingredients that I ordered were kept in the school's warehouse, where rice and other foodstuffs for the student cafeteria were stored. Even though our school's buildings were built using western construction methods as part of a USAID development assistance program in the '60s, rodents had inevitably made their way into the warehouse. A specific rat (of the species *Mastomys natalensis*) common to Lofa County was the prime carrier of the Lassa virus, which was spread by feces and urine contamination of stored grain. I was vaguely aware that several of our school's laborers, who received a portion of their pay in sacks of rice, had been ill with the Lassa fever, and that a Centers for Disease Control (CDC) team was investigating the virus in Lofa County.

I was consumed with leading the students in food preparation and trying to adhere to a tight schedule (something strange to Liberians, who have a more relaxed sense of time). As graduation day approached, I was stressed and exhausted. Finally, the day prior to graduation, a headache, fever, and fatigue landed me in bed, just as Peace Corps staff visited our school to negotiate final details for its use as a training site for incoming volunteers.

Fortunately, the PC training director took pity on me. The next thing I knew, I lay in the back seat of her vehicle, bumping for five hours over bad roads to a private hospital in Monrovia. My only thought was how very lucky I was to enjoy space to stretch out and not be crammed in the back of an overcrowded pickup truck with chickens and goats, and a driver stepping on the brakes to shove everyone and everything forward to fit "just one more" into the rear of the truck.

I was hospitalized for three weeks over Christmas, alone in a foreign country. I was sick as a dog and couldn't keep down medication to control the headache and fever. Hospital doctors were unable to diagnose or successfully treat me. One of my lingering memories is feeling filthy and wanting a bath after days of sweating in bed; I crept slowly down the hallway without assistance, grabbing on to walls and door frames as I made my way to the bathroom at the far end of the hall. Throughout my hospital stay I never lost hope, always thinking that the next day, I would improve.

I later learned that the reason I had no visitors while hospitalized was because of Dr. Paul Mertens, a USAID researcher who stopped in to examine me after he'd heard that a Lofa volunteer was hospitalized. He took one look at the rash on my face and body, guessed it was Lassa, and spread the word that no one was to visit. He knew that approximately fifteen to twenty percent of patients hospitalized with Lassa fever died from the illness. No one told me anything.

After a few weeks (and twenty pounds lighter), I recovered enough to be discharged. Once I was moved to the Peace Corps staff house, Dr. Mertens reappeared to draw a blood sample that he sent to the CDC in Atlanta. When it came back positive for Lassa antibodies, PC wanted to wait to make sure I was not contagious before flying me to D.C. to be checked out. Rumors abounded, and I was told that the airlines and Liberian government were refusing to allow me on a plane. A few weeks later, I flew to D.C., and thankfully, during a thorough exam at the National Institutes of Health, was found to be healthy. I suffered no lingering ill effects; NIH researchers declared my recovery to be the result of my own strong constitution.

I returned to ZTI for my final year of teaching and suffered my headmaster's wrath. He blamed me for the Peace Corps' decision to use a different training site rather than take the risk of exposing new trainees to Lassa fever. Still, I enjoyed teaching my students, built camaraderie with fellow teachers, and had a great volunteer experience.

Two years later, the U.S. Army's Medical Research Institute of Infectious Diseases somehow found me in Minnesota and recruited me to donate plasma on a biweekly basis to provide antibodies to support their biodefense research; at the time, it was thought that the Lassa virus might be used as a biological weapon. After a year of plasma donations, USAMRIID's research director invited me to tour their facility in Ft. Detrick, Maryland., and I "met" (through heavy glass) one of the spacesuit-garbed researchers who had been given my antibodies after a lab accident and potential virus exposure. She gave me a hug through the glass. Journey completed.

Judy Marcouiller was a Peace Corps home economics teacher at Zorzor Rural Teacher Training Institute in Liberia from 1977 to 1979. Following Peace Corps service in Botswana, she worked with Peace Corps recruitment and was a Peace Corps staff member in Sierra Leone and Swaziland. She retired in 2014 after twelve years in the Foreign Service and lives in Minneapolis with Don Garner, her RPCV husband.

RAINY SEASONS (1982)

BY JOHN W. MILLER

Before I joined the Peace Corps
I knew the beat.
I jived and jammed to Jimi,
Aretha, Marvin,
The Stones, The Beatles.
But I didn't know the beat.
Not really.
Not till I woke
one morning in Liberia.

The beat was there.
In Liberia.
In rainy season.
A West African downpour hammering
on roofs of zinc
slammed out restless samba rhythms
while I'd wait for it to stop.

Up the path to Pleebo Town
it was the pound-pound-pound
of palm nuts in the wooden pestle
or boiled cassava beaten into fufu.

The beat was always there.
You could hear it in the gruff
bark-bark of a mottled dog,
all bones,
one ear stripped raw
and limp,
stumbling gamely through
some football with the kids.

The beat was there,
at high school football games,
with spry, grey-haired
Headmaster Nyeka
on the pitch
in trench coat and tie,
shaking his umbrella
at the clouds, while
prancing in a mummer's
strut to celebrate
a goal.

The beat was there
in one backyard,
where two giggling
genius girls
turned crazy twists
of tangled wire
into wheels and axles
fastened onto two crumpled
fish cups,
rescued from a puddle.

Next day, their tiny
race cars, red
and green,
went barreling past
me down the dirt
road into town.

And it was there
in packed-tight
money-buses,
tarps pulled down,
keeping out the mud
and dust,
while the bus
barreled down the
muddy highway.
And me, breathing in
the beat of all the
endless stories
all the way
to Harper Town.

The beat was there
in silent houses
falling with the rain,
their wood ribs showing
where the mud
had gone.

It was there, too,
in stormy twilight,
pounding silent
out of one dark
homestead lighted
only by
a tie-dyed
pink-green
bedsheet hanging
on the porch.

The beat of Liberia
is here.
In me.
I hear it now.
Always.

Calling.
Calling.
Calling
to me.

The June rain
patters gentle
on the glass,
while memory
hammers out a
ceaseless ding-ding
on the corrugated
cover of
my restless
heart.

John Miller served as a Peace Corps volunteer in Liberia from 1981 to 1984 in Maryland County, where he taught English at Pleebo High School. John later served as assistant Peace Corps director for Peace Corps Ukraine from 1993 to 1996. He now teaches cross-cultural communication for the Air Force. His experiences as a PCV provide examples of effective—and ineffective—intercultural communication.

HOLLYWOOD AND VINE

BY MERRIE DUNHAM NEED

In August of 1971, six of us Peace Corps volunteers, serving as teachers in Sanniquellie, Nimba County, Liberia, climbed Mount Soh together. We planned to picnic at a natural shelter created by a giant sandstone boulder that had fallen onto supporting rocks eons earlier. We were young enough to believe we were invincible and all slightly amazed that we were in Africa at all. This combination of perspectives led to some questionable, even hazardous choices.

Standing on the powdery dirt floor of the shelter under the rock, looking down the slope, we saw an abandoned farm that was once machete-slashed and laid bare to the sun in order to grow hill rice. Now it lay fallow, overgrown with lush green twigs and leaves that disguised three-foot, pike-sharp stumps, which farmers had sliced diagonally downward in their haste to "make farm." To our right on the slope, a giant mahogany tree with buttress roots framed our view of the farm below. A tempting vine—a classic Tarzan-type rope—hung from the tree, chest-high and within easy reach.

DH, a former baseball player with formidable upper-body strength, grasped the vine with both hands and rode it in a wide pendulum swing. The slope fell away from him as he sailed forth. It was exhilarating to watch. He returned to the starting point and landed safely, then did it again.

I considered doing exactly what DH had just done. All other vertical vines I had seen in any forest in Liberia could not be similarly ridden because innumerable other vines grew horizontally from tree to tree. Tarzan would have wrapped himself around one of those horizontal vines within ten feet of any takeoff on a vertical one. Authenticity aside, who wouldn't want to swing on a vine like Tarzan when in Africa?

DH handed over the vine for me to try. As I gripped it, I did not feel strong. In fact, I wondered just where my adrenaline had fled. DH told me much later that he didn't rely solely on his grip, but also on the power of his upper arms and shoulders. Unfortunately, this advice came much too late.

DH saw my hesitation but misinterpreted it. "It will hold," he assured me. "I weigh a hundred and seventy-five pounds, and it held for me."

Now you've done it, I thought. If I walk away after that comment, all the Sanniquellie Peace Corps volunteers will assume I weigh more than a hundred and seventy-five pounds. So, I immediately pushed off.

Halfway out, my grip slid an inch downward and then three inches more. There simply wasn't enough vine left below my clasped hands for this to happen again. I chose to stay on as long as I could, hoping I would fall off after the zenith of the swing where each nanosecond would bring me closer to the ground. That was precisely when I remembered that Jane held onto Tarzan, not a vine, whenever she traveled with him.

I managed to stay with the vine past the zenith but fell off a third of the way back. As a skier, I knew to avoid entangling my legs in any fall, so I automatically thrust my legs to the side intending to land on my thigh. I thrust the hand that left the vine first to the side, leaving the hand that last gripped the vine pointing straight up with fingers still furled where the vine once had been. Spectators by the shelter reported that I descended very gracefully for about twenty feet in a sort of gymnastic pose. That comment did not assuage my wounded pride.

I expected to break branches with my body on my way down. Instead, leaves and twigs rose all around me just out of reach. I expected to impale myself on the mini-spikes of machete-slashed saplings below, but that didn't happen. Providentially, I fell through a vertical tunnel created in the high bush by a large, smooth sloped rock. That rock stopped my fall so abruptly that my gold, wire-rimmed, Peace Corps-issued glasses, which wrapped around my ears, flew off upon impact. I rested on the side of my leg and ran a mental inventory of my body starting at my toes. I checked limbs, torso, neck, and head for the pain of injury. When I realized that I was not in pain anywhere except my soon-to-be-purple thigh, I giggled hysterically.

As I sobered up, I risked movement, twisting toward the slope and upward toward the rock shelter. Even with uncorrected myopia, I could see DH standing a third of the way down the slope in a hands-on-hips stance, peering through enough green stuff to locate what he presumed to be my fractured body. I called to him, saying I was all right, but could he help me find my glasses?

In town that night, a volunteer who had not joined the hike said, "I heard you made quite an impression on Mount Soh today."

I responded indignantly, "That is just not true. I landed on a large, smooth rock, leaving no impression at all."

However, what is true is that Liberia made an indelible impression on me, but one, fortunately, that did not take the form of a permanent, physical injury.

Merrie Dunham Need served as an English teacher in the public high school in Sanniquellie, Liberia (1970 to 1972). She became a reading specialist after returning to the U.S., and, twenty years later, an Episcopal priest. Now retired, she and her husband reside in Denver, often visiting her grandson and family in Alaska.

GONLEYEN THE BIRD CATCHER

BY VINCE COSTELLO

At first I didn't think much of it; I just figured he was a good shot. But when it happened two days in a row I was amazed. How had Gonleyen killed fifteen birds in two hours with a slingshot?

I had just finished watering the vegetables in my garden. Tired and with an empty bucket in hand, I headed back to the house to fix dinner and came across Gonleyen returning from the bush. Gonleyen is a Mano name meaning "a man who always steps up to the job." He carried his vine of small birds strung together through the lower mandible like fish on a stringer through their gills. Fourteen of the birds were the same species, the green bulbul, a dull green swamp-lover with no outstanding characteristics. One was a colorful bird of comparable size unknown to both of us. Using *The Birds of West Africa*, we matched it as a white-bellied kingfisher. I told him I'd like to go with him sometime to see how he did it. He said he'd call me the next time he went hunting.

Three days later, he came to my house in the afternoon. I brought my neighbor Sensee's slingshot just to get a feel for the hunt and promised to be quiet. We headed for the bush.

Gonleyen was short for sixteen years old, but muscular. His face had patches of lighter skin where the epidermis had peeled away due to a fungal infection. His little brother, Gongeluo, trailed us, carrying a small black pot of water with leaves covering the top to prevent splashing. I picked up some marble-sized pieces of rock, put them in my pocket and took a few practice shots. I was not on target. It had been almost a dozen years since I had fired one of these gadgets and I didn't remember ever having hit anything, at least not anything that I was aiming for. I wondered how he did it.

Then I noticed he didn't even have a slingshot with him today. I asked him where it was and he said he had given it to his friend. Things weren't making any sense. I asked him how we were going to shoot birds without slingshots? He reassuringly told me, "Just wait and see."

We walked down the main path for a quarter of a mile and then followed an obscure trail through the bush. We reached a stream. It looked like something was about to happen. But what?

In a little clearing among the palms and bamboo, a fire had been started where evidently one had burned before. The leaves were removed from the top of the pot and the pot set in place above the flames. It was difficult to be quiet, so I desperately tried to amuse myself by slinging pebbles at cotton trees, considering a hit any place on the trunk to be a bull's-eye.

Gonleyen reached into the boiling water and removed a glob of solidified latex that he said his father had gathered from a special vine in the bush, and which, when warmed, becomes soft, stretchable, and deathly sticky. He wet his hands to touch it and after three tests decided it was finally ready and the hunt could begin. I still wasn't exactly sure what he had in mind.

At the stream, he had a peeled stick about three feet in length around which he wound his rubberized "fly-paper," and then stuck the stick in the ground at an angle where it extended out over the water. He placed another where the stream turned to the right, and then more sticks farther down along the water's edge, until twelve had been set, always remembering to wet his hands before touching the stickum. In ten minutes, the last trap was in place. We turned around and walked back to the beginning, already having caught two birds.

The scheme was ingenious. The birds would come to drink and bathe. The traps were the seemingly perfect perch. But once the bird landed, it panicked as it tried to escape. Its struggle for survival paradoxically led to its death, as it became more and more stuck.

The method of execution was simple and quick. Gonleyen held the birds in both hands with their head facing his body, and with thumbs pressed firmly against the bird's abdomen, forced the insides out through the anus. It looked painless. In Mano the term for this kind of dead bird translates as "the bird has no poo-poo."

In two hours' time we had fifteen birds and we walked together back to our village, Zahn Zayee. Gonleyen invited me over to his house to sample our catch. Hot coals were already burning at their outdoor firepit and he placed two birds on a grill directly above the coals. The feathers were quickly burned off and after a few rotations the birds were ready for an afternoon snack. They were delicate enough that we could even eat many of the smaller bones. These birds were much scrawnier than chickens, but they were an important addition to a protein-poor diet and helped considerably to thicken the soup.

Perhaps it sounds like a cruel way to put food on your plate, but it certainly was more effective than trying to ruffle the feathers of birds with a slingshot. And, it was ingenious. I felt lucky Gonleyen had shared his secret.

Vince Costello worked as a Peace Corps volunteer in health education in Zahn Zayee, Nimba County, Liberia, from 1978 to 1980. He also taught elementary math and science. Later, he earned a master's in environmental health and worked for twenty-six years in conservation in Hawaii. He lives with his wife and her family in Japan, where he gardens, runs, and is learning Japanese.

ENCHANTING HIGH FOREST LIVING

BY BETTE MCCRANDALL

Some of my more memorable experiences during my Peace Corps years were staying overnight in rural landlocked villages in Lofa County as a member of Curran Lutheran Hospital's Vaccination Team. Among the more outstanding ones was the trip that included the town of Masawo.

In the 1970s, so many of the villages off the main road were still not accessible by car. That meant to get to these villages you had to use the only available transport, the "Leg-2." The jeep went as far as it could go on the road and dropped off the team. We grabbed our loads and started tramping down the bush road on our Leg-2.

The bush road, or path, connected one village to another. It was a regular network of well-maintained pathways as each village was responsible to brush, or cut back, the vegetation on the sides of the bush road halfway to the next village. The distance to any village was measured in how long it took to walk there. (Not to brag, but I could walk just as fast as the locals.)

It was a pleasure to walk on the bush road on hot days. The high forest kept us cool and shaded from the sun. Even if there was a cleared area from a farm from the previous year or two or a clearing for a new rice farm, the farmer could not clear the bush right up to the bush road. The sound of the bush was mostly silence, now and then birds chirped in the canopy. There was no need to be on the lookout for wild animals, but we had to be aware of what could be on the ground: sticks or roots to trip on or even worse—driver ants! It was advisable to stomp our feet and run like hell until clear of those ants. They had pincers, so if they happened to clamp onto your skin, it hurt plenty-o! Snakes? They were a rarity.

Crossing a body of water wasn't a problem. Some kind of bridge spanned the streams: one log, or two-to- three logs tied together. Maybe handrails, maybe not. Some bridges challenged my balancing ability. (No, I never fell off a log bridge but I came close a couple of times—taking a hold of someone's hand was very helpful.) But I loved the vine "monkey" bridges hanging above rivers. A swaying, swinging monkey bridge did not frighten me at all! I trusted that it was well-built and securely fastened, so I wasn't afraid to cross. However, a few of my Liberian colleagues were afraid to cross since many could not swim. Why was the trip to Masawo so special? There were four monkey bridges to cross!

When we were nearing the village, there was always that one last hill to climb before entering. I did not appreciate the climb to the village's center after the long sweaty trek on the bush road, but I knew I had reached our destination. It was protocol to report to the village chief as he was responsible to lodge and feed strangers. After accommodations were settled, I took an opportunity to look around.

There were houses and huts scattered about in no particular pattern, reason, or rhyme. It was as if "house" seeds had been broadcast in every direction. Where they landed, a house or hut grew up. The round hut was typically the "women's quarters" for the chief's wives. Families occupied rectangular houses. It was rare to see window glass. Shutters were used instead to close the window openings. Most of the roofs, once thatch, were zinced by then. That meant zinc sheets had been "head carried" by people from where the zinc was dropped off on the road all the way to the village. The houses were mostly made from mud brick rather than concrete blocks. The palaver hut was located in the center of the village—a round structure with a thatched roof and no sides, only poles, to hold up the roof. A low wall of maybe three-to-four courses of mud bricks provided seating for the important meetings held there. Weather permitting, the palaver hut was a great place for the team to give vaccinations.

I was always given comfortable accommodations, but never had the pleasure of indoor plumbing. No electricity, either, only kerosene lanterns. So where did I take baths? All the houses had a bath fence or bathhouse constructed from sticks or poles stuck into the ground. A *lappa*, a piece of cloth about two yards long, was draped over a stick placed above the opening. This served as the door and provided some privacy. The bath fence was roofless. How beautiful it was to take a warm "bucket bath" under the stars. Stones placed on the floor of the bath enabled water to drain away. I was told I could "pass water" in the bath fence. Remember, no indoor plumbing!

Oh, I can still taste the food! Rice and soup cooked over a wood fire: greens, *kittilee*, bush meat, fish, palm oil, pepper. Too sweet-o! *Kittilee* dry rice for breakfast. I enjoyed eating the Liberian way with the team. (No, I didn't eat with my hand—I was too messy at it!) All the rice and soup were dumped onto a big tray and stirred in together. We stood around the tray, and, each with a spoon in hand, we claimed our "territory" and dug in for a very delicious meal.

The children were so precious. For many, they had never seen a *wekwelege* (white person) before and were curious. While the more timid children hung back, the braver ones got close to touch my skin, my hair, hold my hand. No, I wasn't a *genii* (ghost). But there was a child or two who was definitely deathly scared of me. I felt bad to see a child running to safety, even screaming in fear.

During the day, the village was fairly quiet as most of the people were on their farms. Toward late afternoon, when people started to return, the village came alive with activity: smoke rising from wood fires. The evening meal was being cooked. After eating, people walked about to visit one another. On nights with a bright moon, even the children were out playing and dancing or singing. As it got later, quiet slowly covered the village. Everyone went home to bed, only to be awakened by crowing roosters at five-thirty the next morning.

Bette A. McCrandall served as a Peace Corps volunteer from 1973 to 1978, teaching at Zorzor Central High School. She later remained in Liberia as a teacher and secretary. From 1984 to 2011, she served as a missionary with the Evangelical Lutheran Church in America, working as executive secretary to the bishop and supervisor of the Lutheran Church in Liberia's schools.

FOREST SOUNDS

BY KELLEY MCCREADY

The gentle slap of the screen door against a door frame. The soft shuffle of feet on the dusty ground. Quiet murmurs of voices and a sudden short laugh as the women of the house next door moved about their yard as they began the chores of the day. A barking dog. These were the sounds I heard when I awoke on a good day. On a bad day, the rooster crowed first.

I lived in Kolahun village, high in the rain forest in the northwest interior of Liberia. In early 1973, I had been a Peace Corps volunteer for a year on an assignment with the government's rural development program. On this particular day, I was returning to the neighboring village of Kiantahun for the first time in more than a month.

I had been working with the villagers for almost five months to build a small three-room school. I loved this project and worked particularly hard on it. After a strong start, with the foundation laid and the walls put up in good time, the project stalled. Men who came regularly to work stopped coming. Things had been going so well. I didn't understand what had gone wrong. Though I was a curious person, I also knew my natural reticence got in the way of understanding all that happened around me. The subtleties of the culture often eluded me, and I was sometimes perplexed by the everyday rhythms of how and why things got done. Even so, I couldn't figure out what had happened with the school project. *Probably just some screw-up*, I thought. Finally, I decided to talk with my friend, Mollay Jallah, the old town chief.

Jallah listened intently as I shared my confusion and frustration. Then, smiling, the town chief nodded and said, "Yes, you did do something wrong. The men watch you work and believe you will make sure the building is completed, so they decided they didn't have to try anymore. And you know, when the school building is complete, they won't take care of it because they think it is your school and your responsibility. It will just fall down when you leave. This is true, and you must believe me." I was dumbstruck.

"Well, damn," I said. "What should I do now?"

The town chief looked at me patiently and said, "Come back in two days and speak to the men. I will have them all here to listen. Tell them that the building is not yours, that you don't care if it isn't completed, that your children will not use the school, and that your wife and your mother and your father will never see it. Tell them that you will not come back to Kiantahun until they are ready to work. Then, get in your truck and leave. Wait for them to come and get you. And be patient; it will take some time."

A few days later, I did as Jallah advised. I spoke and the men grew quiet. When I was done, I thanked them, got in my truck, and drove away. And I waited. Four weeks later, some men from the village came to my door in Kolahun. One spoke for all of them. "We are ready for you to come back to work on the school," he said. "And we are ready to work with you."

I was excited but apprehensive on the drive to the village. The thirty-minute drive to Kiantahun was off the main road on a one-lane track that ran straight through the forest. I turned onto the track to the village and my truck was immediately swallowed by thick rain forest. The undergrowth came right up to the edge of the track, scraping the sides as I drove along. The immense old-growth trees formed a leafy canopy high above my head. I drove on a bit, then stopped, turned off the engine, and listened. The silence around me was soon complete.

I wasn't sure what I would find when I reached Kiantahun. Sensing I might be disappointed, I did something that always gave me joy: I listened to the forest. I waited patiently, and gradually, the silence was broken. First by the smaller birds in the lower growth, flitting about from bush to bush, their chatter hurried and songful. Soon, the animals on the forest floor started to move about, rustling leaves and sticks in their haste to get where they were going. Larger birds higher in the canopy began calling raucously. Then came the unmistakable sound of monkeys squealing and chattering high in the treetops. Soon, the forest was a cacophony of sounds. It was magical.

I drove on to the village, across the log bridge and up the steep hill to the clearing in front of the school building. I turned off the engine and sat looking out the windshield. The building site was a buzz of activity with scores of men working. Since I had last been there, the village men had placed the rafters and hung the doors. I got out of the truck and stood next to the door. The men waved and called out and some, including old man Jallah, walked over, greeted me warmly, and talked about their progress on the school.

Later that afternoon, when many of the men had gone back home to rest or do chores, I hiked up the hilltop behind the school. The hillside beyond had been cleared for a rice farm. I sat down on a rock and listened. Down below, I heard the sound of women singing. They were planting rice, broadcasting seed as they moved across the hillside. Other women walked behind, scraping the dirt to cover the seed. A woman with a beautiful strong voice led their song. She sang out a phrase and the rest of the women answered in perfect, multipart harmony. Back-and-forth they went—call, response, call, response.

I had learned a valuable lesson about working with these kind people. Sometimes, it's not just hard work that gets the job done. Sometimes, it's the work you do around the work that is most important. Behind me, men hammered nails like drums. In front of me, women sang songs they had sung for generations. The lessons of life are as many and varied as the sounds of the forest, and it all seemed just a little bit clearer as I sat on that rock on the hillside above the village at the end of that day.

After college, Kelley McCready served in Liberia in the early 1970s as a rural development coordinator and volunteer leader, then worked stateside as a recruiter and on staff with the Office of Special Services in Washington, D.C. He retired after a long career in human resources management and lives with his wife, Anne—an RPCV herself—in Colorado Springs.

THE ROAD TO WILMONT'S VILLAGE

BY KATHLEEN COREY

I left the teacher's meeting and hurried down the dirt road to the money-bus stop. It was 4:30 p.m., and the last one left at five.

I'd been invited to Wilmont's village for a special celebration. Wilmont was my student and had worked for me since I arrived in Zorzor as a Peace Corps volunteer. He helped with the many tasks that were impossible for me to do while meeting the extremely demanding schedule at Zorzor Central High, where I taught three hundred students a day.

Much of rural Liberia in 1975 had no electricity or running water. Wilmont fetched my drinking water from the river that he boiled and filtered. He shopped daily at the village market, cooked a labor-intensive meal of rice and stew, captured rainwater in barrels from the roof of our house during rainy season, kept our lamps full of kerosene and in good working order, and washed most of my clothes in the river, ironing them with a coal-heated iron. A job such as this received fifteen dollars a month—volunteers received seventy-five dollars—and was highly sought-after, not only because of the money (a large sum in rural Liberia), but because Peace Corps volunteers were known to be kind and caring employers who helped both the student and their families.

I couldn't miss the village celebration—I'd promised Wilmont I would come, and I knew my presence, as a foreigner, would bring honor to his village. It was believed I would bring good luck to them.

I waited for a money-bus at the bend in the road. None came. A downpour suddenly began. As I stood there and night began to fall, a man whose house was near the money-bus stop came out and said he thought that I'd just missed the last one, but that the village wasn't too far by foot. He offered me an umbrella since I was quite soaked in my light rain jacket. Umbrella in hand, I began my walk just as night fell. My clogs I wore to the classroom that day were not suited for this wet dirt road filled with potholes and rocks. By Liberian standards, it was indeed "not very far." By my American standards, it would turn out to be a good two-hour hike.

As darkness fell, the jungle came alive with the sounds of birds and animals cawing and growling. I became afraid. About an hour into my walk, I saw the lights of a money-bus. I jumped out, wildly waving my arms. To my amazement, the vehicle sped past, splashing me with red mud. According to Liberian folklore, the evil spirits of the forest are white. Was that why the money-bus didn't stop?

I kept walking. At one point, I crossed a small river swollen with rain, rushing over the road. One of my clogs slipped off in the rushing water and as I dove to retrieve it, I dropped my umbrella and watched it float away. The sounds of the night became louder, and I wondered at one point if I had to lie down on the side of the road and wait until morning. But what about the poisonous snakes and the driver ants that could kill a person with their bites? No . . . I had to keep going.

Another money-bus approached. This time, I stepped in front of it: I figured I'd rather be hit by this vehicle than eaten by driver ants. The money-bus stopped, and I climbed in the back, sopping wet, sprinkling water drops on the stunned passengers. What a sight I must have been when we arrived: a white woman, wet to the bone and dazed. Word got out that I had arrived, and Wilmont came running up to me, grinning ear-to-ear, as he realized I'd been telling the truth when I'd promised to come. Wilmont's sister also came running and led us to their home, where I waited for a bucket of water to boil over a fire in preparation for a very hot bucket bath. Once warm and clean, I stepped out of the concrete bathhouse wrapped in a big towel to find something lying on the bed of raffia where I would sleep that night. There, lay the most beautiful, hand-embroidered *lappa* dress, something a Liberian bride would wear.

Dressed in my exquisite Liberian outfit, Wilmont escorted me to the main square where the dancing and drinking were in full swing. As is Liberian custom, I was offered my choice of freshly harvested palm wine, made from the fermented sap of a palm tree, or another favorite Liberian drink—Guinness beer and Coke. I took the palm wine and soon was dancing in one big group next to the "old ma's"—the strong, elderly women who made the village run. People kept touching my wet hair and white skin. I was quite certain I was the first white person they had met. The next day, Wilmont and I rode in the back of a money-bus to Zorzor. The clothes I'd worn the day before had been washed and ironed—I was ready for school.

I felt like a queen the entire time I was in Wilmont's village; everyone went out of their way to treat me with such kindness and love. As I rode back to my village, I reflected on the night before and knew even then that this would be one of my life's most memorable experiences.

Years later, I corresponded with a fellow volunteer still living in Liberia, and learned of the struggles Liberians were encountering with food and security due to the civil war. Her letter shocked me to my core when I learned Wilmont had fallen from a palm tree as he was gathering coconuts for his hungry family. Wilmont died in the fall.

Despite my sadness over the loss of such a wonderful person, I will always remember the road to Wilmont's village, and the joy on his face when I finally made it there.

Kathleen Corey was a Peace Corps volunteer in Zorzor, Liberia, and volunteer leader from 1975 to 1979. She is currently the President of Women of Peace Corps Legacy. She also served as Peace Corps country director for North Macedonia and Sri Lanka, regional director of Asia and Pacific, chief of operations for Pacific, Asia, Central and Eastern Europe, and a diplomat and NGO leader.

MY PANGOLIN

BY KAREN E. LANGE

The foot-and-a-half-long creature hanging by its tail from my houseboy's arm was covered in scales, with a long, flicking tongue and eyes like little black beads. Abraham stood at the front door of the house where I lived in Belefanai (a town in northern Liberia) holding the animal out to me like a gift.

"That ant bear," Abraham said. "It for you." He smiled as though I should be happy.

I thought of the injured bird he had brought me not so long before. After a few weeks I found a pile of feathers. My cat had eaten her. I wasn't ready to take on another doomed pet. "How will I feed it?" I asked.

"That ant bear," said Abraham. "It can eat ants."

"Yeah, but how am I going to find ants every day, every day?"

"We will help you. Me and the *pekins*." (Liberian English for small child.) He spoke sincerely. But Abraham, fifteen, was barely present to do his chores. He had been assigned to me by his uncle, my landlord, to haul water and wash my more rugged clothes with a piece of lye soap on a rock in a nearby swamp. Now that I had paid his school fees and advanced him money for a bicycle, our relationship had shifted. I was like a mother. And he, like a wayward son. Often I would find the jars of American peanut butter I splurged on in Monrovia scraped nearly clean soon after purchase. "Empty bag can't stand," said the ever-hungry Abraham.

As for the *pekins*, a band of children from my landlord's extended family, our relationship had not developed much beyond when I first arrived in 1984 as a Peace Corps fisheries volunteer and they hung over the windowsills to stare at me, or ran away, giggling, as I came out of the house, crying *"Kwii kolle! Kwii kolle!"* (White woman! White woman!)

"No, this one not like dog. It not like cat. It lives in the forest. It for you," said Abraham once more. "This one baby. They coming to eat the mother. The meat sweet-o."

So I took the ant bear. She seemed friendly. Although her back and tail were armored, she had a pink-skinned, white-furred underbelly and was attracted to the warmth of my skin. She climbed onto my arm, her long claws grasping but not scratching. When I put her down on the floor of my house, she pulled her way up my leg as though it were a tree trunk. With some difficulty—she was muscular—I removed her and placed her in a cardboard box with dirt and a container of water so I could go search for ants. She curled into a ball and went to sleep. The cat examined her curiously but could do her no harm.

That first day I found the ants just a hundred feet beyond the yard of my house in a dusky tower of gray dirt they had built on the edge of the forest. I brought the ant house back and broke it up with a machete. The ant bear's tongue flicked out to catch the little creatures and their white eggs. She seemed content. *Flick. Flick.* I watched her eat with deep satisfaction.

As the days went by, though, it became harder and harder to find ants. I looked into the stand of trees as I drove my motorbike on the dirt roads to teach an algebra class or visit farmers I was helping raise fish in ponds. Abraham did his chores hurriedly and rushed off before I could ask about ants. The *pekins* for once were neither seen nor heard.

I grew worried about my ant bear. She showed so much affection, although I suspected it was just instinct for her to cling to one or the other of my legs. I had not named her, but I was starting to love her. The cat had developed a sort of friendship with her, too. They would touch noses. But how would my ant bear eat?

Concerned that she was not getting enough food, I began to examine her more closely. I saw beneath her scales rows and rows of brown bumps. They looked like mites or ticks. I worried they would make her sick or weak. I wanted to get the parasites off to quickly fix the problem. What I did next is hard to explain in hindsight: I had no reference book. The nearest phone was twenty miles away. My only contact with the outside world was the weekly Peace Corps mail truck. And I was very young—just out of college with a bachelor's and a few months' training, but little practical experience of the cause and effect of life. Impulsively, I got a can of insecticide—the kind I used to drive back waves of cockroaches—and aimed the aerosol spray at the skin under her scales.

That night, the ant bear was listless. I did not have any ants, so I could not tell if she had lost her appetite. But all at once, I realized what I had done: The insecticide had soaked through her skin, poisoning her. There was no veterinarian in the town. No doctor. No pharmacy. The USAID-built clinic had no drugs. I looked in my Peace Corps medical kit—the one that when I first arrived I had used to bandage the festering wound of a man who came to me after slicing open his arm with a cutlass—and took out a packet of powder for oral rehydration solution. I found a pair of worn-out corduroy pants and made a bed for her. Then, not knowing what else to do, I offered her water with the powder dissolved in it. Hoping her tongue was taking in liquid, I stayed up with her for hours. In the morning, she was dead.

As the sun was coming up through the trees, and the air turned warm enough to make me sweat, I went into the backyard with a shovel and the ant bear wrapped in the pants. Abraham found me digging a hole.

"The ant bear dead-o," he said.

I nodded, ashamed that rather than keeping the little creature alive I had killed it. "I coming to bury it."

"I will dig," he said, and took the shovel from my hands.

When the hole was a couple feet deep, he stopped and I picked up the shrouded ant bear to place her in. Delicately, Abraham asked, "You will bury the pants also?" He was wearing torn shorts.

Feeling foolish, I unwrapped the ant bear and handed Abraham the corduroys. "No, I will not bury the pants."

Then, I lay the ant bear to rest, laughing that Abraham's concern was for the pants, crying for the ant bear. I had been in Liberia many months as a Peace Corps volunteer: deferred to because I was American; expected to solve problems and provide answers; impatient sometimes with the way Liberians just accepted things; respected, and yet separate from everyone around me. That morning, the lonely burden of the illusion that I could always fix things was lifted. I was just a flawed and fallible human being who had chosen the exact wrong thing to do. Humbled by failure and filled with regret.

Karen E. Lange served as a Peace Corps volunteer in Belefanai from 1984 to 1986. After witnessing the rigged election and attempted coup of 1985, she became a journalist. She returned to Liberia as a journalist and also a Friends of Liberia elections observer. Her husband, Stuart Gagnon, traveled there with her during the war. Her two children hope to travel there someday.

IN THE HOSPITAL THEY KILL PEOPLE

BY MARTIN FORD

During my Peace Corps volunteer years in Liberia, I had two direct encounters with a hospital. The first was a positive experience. Part of my training was in Ganta, which had a hospital where I sought treatment for a sprained ankle. A nurse took my temperature and blood pressure. A doctor asked a few questions and manipulated the joint. I left on crutches with my ankle wrapped in an ace bandage and a doctor's admonitions to rest, elevate, and ice it. Care was much like it would have been in the U.S.

My next encounter was more complicated. It occurred in 1976, during my second year of teaching. By then, I had learned that Liberians could be ambivalent about Western medicine. In class, a student had even said that he would never go to a hospital, because, "In the hospital they kill people." I was incredulous and tried to change his mind. It was my next hospital visit that helped me understand why this student felt the way he did.

On the first day of school, I asked other teachers about a new student I had noticed at recess, Moses—a boy whose cheek protruded under his eye, pushing his nose to one side. My colleagues told me it was not a tumor. It was a hard growth under his skin. Everyone said it had grown larger in recent months. I consulted with my principal, and we decided to go to Moses' home one evening to ask his parents if I could take him to the hospital to have his condition checked out. They agreed.

The morning of our trip, Moses turned out in his Sunday best. He was nervous but excited. The dry season ride to the hospital was routine. In the 1970s that meant more than a dozen people packed into the back of a canopied compact pickup truck (money-bus) with goats, chickens, and luggage bumping over rough dirt roads. After we arrived, we walked to the hospital along a road lined with majestic palms. It was only after entering the hospital grounds that the visit began to turn badly.

Along the front walk, patients sat on shaded benches under the palm trees. The hospital had been built decades earlier as a treatment center for lepers. Leprosy, or Hansen's disease, is much rarer than in the old days and is eminently treatable. If caught early, it need not result in physical deformity. Yet, Ganta was a center for patients who required reconstructive surgery, prosthetic shoes, and physical therapy. Some had come from other parts of the country years before but chose not to return home because of the stigma of the disease.

As Moses and I walked past the benches, he took my hand. He was scared. It was mostly leprosy patients sitting on the benches, many of them older and bearing such telltale markers as facial lesions, deformed noses, and missing fingers and toes. Visitors ran a visual gauntlet that gave a distorted picture of the benefits of a hospital stay.

Once in the hospital, our wait was short. A tall Sudanese doctor gave Moses a full physical before calling in an American colleague. The two examined Moses' face, which they palpated thoroughly. Throughout, I remained near to help put Moses at ease. But clearly the encounter unnerved him. I had not warned him the exam would involve him undressing and that strange men would prod him and murmur to each other. These are things we Americans begin to experience from our first visit to the pediatrician, but they were new to Moses.

During this examination, I overheard one doctor ask the other, "Burkitt's?" Before I learned the answer to that cryptic question, we were directed to a bench in a sunny hallway in a lightly trafficked section of the hospital and instructed to wait. The doctors needed to confer. We'd been there for only five minutes when an orderly emerged from a room pushing a gurney, bearing a woman who lay on her side, covered partly with a sheet. The orderly left her. I recall looking at the woman's bare back. Her skin looked lustrous in the sun. She didn't seem to be breathing. She wasn't.

The next thing I knew, Moses grabbed my arm. He, too, noticed the woman's lifeless body. It was only a minute before the orderly returned with other staff. There was a flurry of activity around the body. We were called back to the doctor. He briefed me on a malady called "Burkitt's lymphoma." Rare outside of Africa, Burkitt's lymphoma is found overwhelmingly among children who have contracted malaria. The doctor said it was incurable and rapidly fatal if untreated. The good news was that it was treatable.

I explained to Moses the best I could. If he could live near the hospital, he would be provided medication that would slow the growth of his tumor. A Peace Corps friend, Scott, who lived in Ganta, was impressed by Moses' congeniality. He offered to take the boy in to ensure that he took his medicine and would enroll him in the school where Scott was teaching. While this was hardly the cure we had hoped for, it beat the inexorable physical decline that the doctors predicted for Moses were he to go untreated.

When we returned to the village, I explained the course of action to the school's principal, and we again visited Moses' family. They were naturally upset by the doctor's prognosis but agreed that his moving to Ganta and living near the hospital was for the best.

The following Monday, Moses did not show up for school. In fact, he never showed up again. Moses had run away. Whether he went to relatives living in Monrovia or further "into the bush," I never learned. The experience brought back to me my student's complaint, "In the hospital they kill people!"

Martin Ford was a Peace Corps volunteer in Gblor Dialah (1975 to 1976) and Ganta (1976 to 1977). He taught language arts and science in middle school and high school. Martin went on to complete a doctorate in anthropology as a Fulbright researcher in Liberia (1985 to 1986). He retired as Associate Director of the Maryland Office for Refugees and Asylees in 2014.

THE HEADPAN PALAVER: THE PROCESS OF DEVELOPMENT

BY JUDY SCHROEDER

I arrived in Liberia in late 1981 as part of a small group of Appropriate Technology Peace Corps volunteers, and I was assigned to the village of Warsonga in the Kissi Chiefdom of Lofa County. My role was to combine needs-based community development with the design of small-scale technological innovations appropriate to the people's lives—i.e., appropriate technology. As a step in this process, it was important for me to hear directly from the women in order to better understand the community's needs and priorities—since they often didn't participate in larger community discussions typically managed by men. I initiated a series of Women in Development meetings to give village women an opportunity to provide input on the types of projects they would like to undertake in their community.

One Women in Development gathering was especially memorable. On a Sunday evening in May, about ten women arrived at the colorfully painted, open-air palaver hut for our weekly meeting. Wango Kumba, the Women's chief, sat directly in front of me and spoke with Josephine, my counterpart and translator, while we waited for more women to arrive. I contented myself with watching the chief, admiring her beauty, strength, power, and pride—Wango Kumba's stature seemed to be symbolized by her multicolored, intricately designed, batik *lappa* dress and matching head scarf. The women came. The meeting began.

Women in Development stove-building project, 1982

Fifteen minutes later, a major palaver (a heated argument) ensued regarding the women who had not shown up for the meeting. Unbeknownst to me, Wango Kumba had issued an order for her deputy to go and check all of the houses in the village to see if any women remained inside. If they found one, a small pan was to be collected from the missing woman and carried to the palaver hut.

The chief's deputy entered with a gigantic "headpan" and proceeded to set it down in the middle of the large, round concrete floor. I didn't think this out of the ordinary: Women walked around everywhere with these large, enameled basins balanced on their heads to carry heavy loads of produce from the farm or food from the market. It was now dark in the palaver hut, so I couldn't see the many "small-small" pans inside the big one. But, instantly upon the deputy's arrival, the assembly of women became unruly, jumping up out of their seats and screaming among themselves. I had no idea what was going on. I grabbed Josephine from the chaos to find out what was happening. She explained, "It went so: One woman got vexed when the deputy took her small pan from her hut. She said they shouldn't punish her for not attending this week because she had come last week. They had never punished others before!"

Another fifteen minutes passed. The Town Chief, Falla Kaasu, was summoned, and he arrived in a vain attempt to calm everyone. He walked over to me and suggested that I could have meetings with the men instead of the women. He said, "The men would all come, be very attentive, and—most importantly—I would be able to control them. I have no power over these women!" Falla Kaasu got frustrated and retreated, shaking his head in resignation.

The female palaver continued. Wango Kumba was back in charge. She got vexed and walked out of the palaver hut, steaming, cooled off, came back for a couple of minutes, then got vexed again. A decision was finally made. Next week, one woman would be appointed to stand at the palaver hut entrance to collect a fine of twenty-five cents from anyone who would dare to disrupt the meeting. Of course, this choice of action, like that of collecting the pans, was done entirely in the local Kissi language, which I was just beginning to learn.

Then Josephine explained the group's decision to me. I replied, "I don't approve of the idea of using force to hold a meeting."

Josephine argued that the measures taken were basically empty threats, and they were the only way to get people in the village to cooperate. As the women departed, a few said that the old women should all be banned from coming to the meetings, because they were the ones who caused the palaver in the first place.

I went home, put on my shorts, selected a cassette of vintage Dylan, and peacefully washed the day's dishes. I was amazed at the evening's events and how daunting and challenging this adventure would be—to work with the women and their communities to help them think about innovative ideas to improve their lives.

This is the process of development.

Judy Schroeder was an Appropriate Technology Peace Corps volunteer in Lofa County's Kissi Chiefdom from 1981 to 1984. Judy managed the Federation of Liberian Youth's Health Animator program, secured Dutch funding for a community water and sanitation project, and trained Lofa County agricultural staff in fuel-saving cook stoves. Judy has worked with global development organizations in Latin America and Asia since earning a master's.

WHAT!! ME *KWE*?

BY BETTE MCCRANDALL

One afternoon in 1976, Jan Olson, a fellow Peace Corps volunteer, and I decided to walk to downtown Zorzor to the center part of town—what we called the Four Corners—just to sit on the curb and people-watch. That area was the busiest part of the city of Zorzor, both daytime and night. Small shops lined the streets in four directions. St. John's Lutheran Church occupied one of the corners. People were walking about, going here and there, into one store, exiting another. Some market women sat at the edge of the road beside their *whee-la*, or market table, selling their small, small goods: candy, cigarettes, ground pea, candles, boxes of matches, and packs of baking soda for *torbogee* soup. Two men sitting outside a store were playing country checkers. Other people were just milling about in small-small groups, talking and looking about. Traffic was not heavy; it only got that way on market days. Occasionally, a vehicle bounced down the dusty road to the center of town: a Curran Hospital jeep, one taxi then another, a money-bus or two.

Most often, the taxis and money-buses picked up their passengers on the main road at the edge of town. However, on this day, a money-bus pulled in and parked near where we were sitting. The money-bus was empty, so the driver had to be looking for passengers. Jan and I continued sitting there, just chitchatting, taking in all the activities around us. If one of my high school students or one of Jan's home arts students happened to see us, they came over to greet us. Otherwise, the local people paid us no attention.

Then, another vehicle pulled up in front of the store across the street to let out passengers. From inside emerged two *wii-kwe-legeuis,* Loma for "white people." Our eyes popped open and we just stared and stared at the strangers—two white men! Liberians who also spied the strangers had the same reaction: to stop and stare.

Who are those white men? Where are they coming from? Where are they going? What are they doing here? We pondered these questions, speculating on a whole bunch of reasons. While Jan and I were discussing and wondering about the two men we saw, I happened to casually glance down at my bare arms.

Hey-ya! What a shock! My arms were the same color as those two *wee-kwe-legeuis!*

I looked up at the men again and back at my bare arms. I had reacted as if I were a Liberian seeing white people for the first time. How had this happened to me just a few years after arriving in Liberia? I had assimilated unknowingly into feeling Liberian on the inside, but I certainly did not look Liberian on the outside.

I was just as *kwe* on the outside as those two men. Hey-ya! What to do?

Bette A. McCrandall served as a Peace Corps volunteer from 1973 to 1978, teaching at Zorzor Central High School. After that, she remained in Liberia as a teacher and secretary. From 1984 to 2011, she served as a missionary with the Evangelical Lutheran Church in America, working as executive secretary to the bishop and supervisor of the Lutheran Church in Liberia's schools.

MAKING A DIFFERENCE

BY DAVID BAUR

The road from my house to the school in Sanniquellie passed in front of the District Commissioner's compound. Several government officials lived in the compound, including the tax collector. In 1964, when another volunteer and I who taught in the same school were leaving, the community had a going-away party for us.

Various people spoke, including the tax collector. "I will remember you boys for one important reason. You boys went to work every day. There were many rainy days when I didn't intend to go to work. But then, as I sat on my porch, I would see you two boys going to work and I would say to myself that if those two boys can go to work, then I should, too."

One aspect of the Peace Corps' experience was that we didn't always know what impact we had on the people of our community or our students. I believe that I helped my students, but I also know that people of the community observed our life in that town. And the tax collector went to work on some rainy days.

David Baur was a Peace Corps volunteer in Sanniquellie, Liberia, from 1962 to 1964. David taught English and biology for grades 7 to 12 in Sanniquellie Central School. David continued teaching in Laos, in a Michigan county jail, and in a refugee language program. David enjoys contra dancing and choral singing. David returned to Sanniquellie with his son in 2012.

PART II
TURBULENT TIMES

GOODBYE, SWEET LIBERIA

BY JEFF CRANE

After suffering through malaria, amoebic dysentery, and tapeworms, I thought my medical woes were behind me. Eighteen months into my two years of service as a health educator in dusty Bahn Town, in the heart of Nimba County, I was hitting my stride: The clinic was running well, vaccination numbers were up, and my health education classes were well-attended. Friendships with Gio and Mandingo villagers, Lebanese merchants, even the Irish missionaries were all flourishing. The new military government of Liberia was trying to establish itself, supplies were once again reaching upcountry, and I started planning travel following my completion of service.

In June 1980, I was finishing a quick trip to Monrovia for some supplies and cash. I was in a hurry to get back to Bahn in order to help with clinic the next day. Traveling at night during the height of the rainy season was never a good idea, but the last money-bus had a space in the front. I tossed the driver the required dollars and climbed into the middle seat of the overflowing Volkswagen van. Passengers, chickens, and a bundled live goat filled the back. An older gentleman and I were wedged in the front with the driver.

Thick clouds moved in and quickly darkened the sky as we headed out. Soon it was thundering, lightning, and pouring rain. I grew sleepy watching the motion of the wipers and began to doze off thinking about how many vaccines I would need for the morning clinic.

Suddenly everybody was screaming. I opened my eyes in time to see another equally overflowing money-bus pull out right in front of us. I remember trying to brace myself against the dashboard as the word "Toyota" smashed into the front of our van. There was a horrid screeching of brakes, an explosion of metal smashing into metal, and then . . . silence.

A dark, steamy heaviness hung over my dream before I came to. Then, I heard screaming again, yelling, and cries of pain. We had flipped on our side and the metal front of the VW van had collapsed against our legs. The driver had managed to wiggle out, and he and several others were pulling on me trying to free me from the wreck. I yelled at them to stop, as I cautiously scanned my injuries. My arms were crunched, my head was split open and bleeding badly, and both bones in my lower left leg were snapped cleanly in two. I gripped my pant leg as tightly as I could and yelled that they were going to have to carry me out in this position because of my broken leg. After several moments of tugging and pulling, they got me out and laid me on the road next to my seatmate.

The driver was crying out in pain and calling on Allah every few breaths. I took note and said a lengthy prayer myself as I realized my nightmare was about to come true: I was going to be admitted as an emergency into a Liberian hospital. Incredibly, though, I was almost calm. Because my body was still in shock, nothing really hurt. I remember continuing my prayer and looking up at the clearing sky, thinking, *This is it. I am going to be medically terminated. I'm going home. Goodbye, sweet Liberia.*

We had crashed outside of Ganta, but their hospital was not equipped to handle the twenty-two victims, so we had to be transported back to the hospital in Gbarnga, forty-three miles away. The only way to do that was to cram us into smaller taxis. They stuck my broken leg out the window and I held on to the pant leg with every ounce of strength I could muster calling on Jesus, Allah, and anyone else who might be available to help.

Triage quickly divided us up, and soon I was x-rayed and wheeled into surgery to have my head sewn up and my leg casted. I remember watching a nurse count out the bloody three hundred dollars from my money belt before locking it up in a safe. After receiving some strong meds, I finally fell asleep mumbling something to someone about contacting the Peace Corps.

I woke up the next morning to a nurse who was trying to saw the plaster cast off my leg because she felt it had been set incorrectly. The doctor came by, made her stop, and reassured me I would be fine. Peace Corps was on its way to pick me up. While I waited, I passed the time flicking the cockroaches off my IV-tube.

Comfort Baker, our chief medical officer, arranged for my transfer to Cooper's Clinic in Monrovia. She then garnered four seats on a flight to Washington, D.C.: one for her and three for me and my plaster friend. I was in D.C. for a week before I was able to fly home to San Francisco.

The entire process of my medical termination, airplane flights, medical care, and therapy in San Francisco was all very efficiently handled by the Peace Corps. Neither my parents nor I ever saw a single medical bill. Despite being upset about my sudden departure from Liberia, the sadness of not being able to say goodbye to so many dear Liberian friends, and the frustration of being in a cast all summer, I was incredibly grateful to be alive and to be home.

My time in Liberia taught me the lifelong values of patience and perseverance. The work and living conditions were never easy, but the unexpected displays of sincere appreciation more than made up for the difficulties I encountered. I may carry scars from the accident, but I will never forget the simple pleasure of a shared bowl of rice, or the gentle touch of an old ma's weathered hand followed by her musical greeting in Gio, *"Aa-oo!"*

Jeff Crane was a Peace Corps volunteer in Bahn Town, Nimba County, Liberia, from 1978 to 1980. He worked as a health educator in the clinic and taught health in the local school. After a two-year teaching assignment in Medellin, Colombia, he and his wife settled down in Arizona, where they taught for the next thirty-six years.

WELCOME TO MONROVIA

BY SARAH CRADDOCK MORRISON

I awoke to the national anthem blaring from loudspeakers across the city and thought I must still be dreaming. "All hail, Liberia, hail! All hail, Liberia, hail! This glorious land of liberty shall long be ours . . ." Was this a regular occurrence? Maybe to get people up and ready for the workday, since most people did not have alarm clocks? I roused sleepily to look out the window, and it seemed that everyone in the neighborhood was already in the street, banging on cook pots, singing, laughing, and dancing for joy. That could not be normal! I watched and listened, trying to understand.

It was November 12, 1985. I had just moved into an apartment in Monrovia to start my Peace Corps assignment as a training and logistics coordinator for a project at the Ministry of Health. I had no telephone or means of communicating with the Peace Corps office to ask what was happening, but I had bought batteries for a transistor radio. All stations were reporting that the government of the Second Republic, under the country's first indigenous president, Samuel Kanyon Doe, had been overthrown, and the Liberian people were "liberated."

I was excited to witness history unfolding, but before I even finished dressing, the radio went silent, and I began to hear lots of gunfire. People celebrating in the street started screaming and running. The welcomed coup d'état had not held. Doe's supporters exacted revenge beyond the reach of laws or protocols. In the coming days, they shot, tortured, "disappeared," and executed many Liberians.

I did not fully understand what was occurring. I remained uneasy, alone in my apartment. Word finally reached me from the Peace Corps office more than twenty-four hours later, saying to stay at home until further notice, so I waited. The following day, I sat on my porch quietly reading in the hot, sticky, early evening.

Suddenly, three furious soldiers ran toward me, screaming something and shaking their M-16s. My vocal cords became paralyzed with fright! I could not get a sound out, though my mouth was wide open. As I leapt from my porch chair, I realized I had no chance of getting inside before they would reach me. I thought maybe I would be safer if I stayed outside. Those curious neighbors might come to my rescue. If I were to open the door, these guys might take the chance to push me inside and do whatever they wanted.

I could smell beer and palm wine on their breaths as they jumped on the porch. They made no sense, but their body language was unmistakable. I was in trouble.

The Alpha soldier screamed, "Shut yur mouf and come wit me or I shoot you for true!"

Was it a bluff? Why did he pick on me? Because I was a white woman, alone? He screamed something about the curfew and how I must be a rebel. However, the recently imposed government curfew required everyone to stay off the *streets*. I was on "my" property—my porch—obviously *not* breaking a curfew!

I stood my ground nervously and breathed deeply, regaining my voice. "What do you want? I am not doing anything wrong!"

Then, the Alpha soldier yanked my arm, and when I screamed in pain, I knew neighbors could hear. I yelled, "Help me!" as loudly as I could.

Rooms were dark inside the apartments across the driveway. Still, the soldiers saw people peeking out and aimed their guns in that direction while screaming something I could not understand that was undoubtedly threatening.

"Call Peace Corps! Tell them they are taking me!" I yelled as the soldiers pulled me off the porch and stuck one of the M-16s in my back while cursing at me. I did not honestly expect my brand new neighbors to be able to help. Who had a phone? Was there even an emergency number for the Peace Corps? Why would they take a risk for me?

It had become dark, and the gunfire got louder as we headed into unlit, vacant streets toward an unknown destination. I had no idea what was around me or what to do, but I did not doubt that they would shoot me if I tried to escape. Then, they could say I *was* breaking curfew. I knew they had orders to shoot any "rebel" on the street.

Did the drunk Alpha soldier who grabbed me expect a large reward for killing a *kwi* woman? It was now pitch dark, and he was leading us on a path through high weeds. Would I be raped? They were so drunk that a gun could misfire and kill any of us if they accidentally tripped. That was perhaps a more realistic threat. I am sure I prayed, but I knew that bad things happened to good people—most Liberians were good people, and how many had died already?

Perhaps the concern my family and friends had expressed when I left a good job and life in the U.S. for a Peace Corps adventure was valid. Here I was before I had even started my assignment, wondering if my life would end.

We stumbled along unlit streets for hours. The soldiers seemed more anxious as they began to sober up, and although I had no cash on me, I promised them what I had at home if they took me back and then left. I was able to convince the soldiers and finally when we returned, I gave them the meager twenty dollars I had. With a treasure equal to at least half a month's pay, they staggered off.

Perhaps that is what they wanted in the first place, and I was too naïve or stubborn to see it. I quickly learned that despite my supposed wisdom and experience, I had to recognize the potential for danger, especially if I did not fully understand the culture. The challenge of the Peace Corps would be more complex than just my choice to do good and experience a less materialistic life.

With an unexpected wake-up anthem and its violent aftermath, my welcome to Monrovia abruptly began.

Sarah Craddock Morrison was a PCV with the Ministry of Health in Monrovia from 1985 to 1987, which changed her career path. She moved to D.C., worked for USAID, passed the Foreign Service exam, and joined the State Department. One of her assignments before retirement included work as a public affairs officer in Monrovia from 1998 to 2001. She is president of Friends of Liberia.

WHICH HOME?

BY KELLEY JEWETT

On November 12, 1985, Thomas Quiwonkpa led an unsuccessful coup attempt against President Samuel Kanyon Doe. I was in the Catholic Hospital in Monrovia recovering from surgery for a severely infected foot when the announcement came over the radio that Quiwonkpa and his men had taken over the Liberian radio station. Not long after that, Doe spoke on the radio, stating that Quiwonkpa had been killed and he was back in power. No one was safe. My nurse informed me that the hospital had to be emptied to make space for people wounded in the fighting. Shortly thereafter, a Peace Corps officer came to pick me up.

I could not return to my village because it was three days away by car, dugout canoe, and foot travel, and because the government prohibited traveling by road. Instead, I was taken to the two-bedroom apartment of a fellow Peace Corps volunteer in Monrovia, where seven other volunteers were also staying. We were forbidden to leave the apartment because the danger was too great. Our Peace Corps officer supplied us with food, water, and other necessities.

The apartment was crowded and we were bored. There were constant sounds of gunfire, and from our windows we saw army dump trucks loaded with bodies to be disposed of in the ocean. Tensions ran high. When our roommate dropped a spoon on the floor, we all jumped. When it was my turn to cook supper and my friend told me the spaghetti was too sticky, I bawled. There was nothing I wanted more than to get back to my village, as I was certain that everything would be normal there.

After about ten days, the Peace Corps gave us permission to go for short walks to buy onions and tomato paste from the nearby stalls. Curfew was at 6 p.m., which meant that we had to be back by five-thirty, lest some drunk, untrained soldier who had received two hundred dollars for joining the army felt the need to detain us until 6 p.m. so he could shoot us. I went to the money-bus station every day to see if any vehicles were going to Harper or Sasstown, which were near my village. At last, I found one. My next step was to get approval from the Peace Corps office. With no reliable communication regarding the dangers outside Monrovia, the Peace Corps staff used the limited information they had and reluctantly allowed me to return to my village.

The road to Harper passed through Zwedru, the hometown of President Doe and an area of high-security checkpoints. Our money-bus broke down and we waited hours for a repairman to come and fix the vehicle. Darkness had set in before we were able to continue. Being on the road during the night was never safe, much less so now.

"Where are you going, white man?" the drunken soldier demanded, though it was obvious I was a woman. He led me into a small room in the back corner of the thatched structure at the checkpoint.

The utter darkness of the forest was broken only by the weak light from a small kerosene lantern on the rickety wooden table. There were no witnesses except the drunken soldier, his machine gun, and me, as he asked to see my ID. I was terrified; he had singled me out as the only white person and a female Peace Corps volunteer on the crowded money-bus. I knew that this soldier could do anything he wanted with me, even kill me, and I would be among those who just disappeared in the night. After harassing me for a short time, the soldier let me go and we proceeded in the darkness.

Two days later, I was overjoyed to arrive at my house in Barclayville. Soon, I discovered many of my fellow teachers and friends had been jailed for nothing other than the crime of belonging to President Doe's opposition party. When I checked on my friends, I found them in a small building with a leaky thatched roof, crammed together with other men lying end-to-end on the dirt floor. They had infected whiplash wounds on their backs, received watery soup once a day, and were never allowed outside. The soldiers allowed me to talk with my friends for a couple of minutes, but after that visit, they did not permit me to return.

For decades, the U.S. had funded Liberia's development through various projects and programs. I learned from a leader in USAID, based in Monrovia, that Doe had diverted some of these well-intended U.S. dollars to fund his crimes against the Liberian people. I was outraged. *Newsweek* magazine, Peace Corps workers' regular connection to the outside world, reported that just six people were killed in the fighting. I knew better, because I saw many dead bodies and destroyed villages on my journey back to Barclayville, not to mention the dump trucks loaded with bodies in Monrovia.

I needed to go home for a couple of weeks at Christmas to determine if I could continue as a volunteer. I struggled with representing my country, which continued to inadvertently fund a regime led by a ruler who had gained his power through a military coup and had no qualms about killing his own people.

While in the U.S., I wrote to my senators and representatives in Washington, D.C., about what was happening in Liberia, and they said they were not aware of the situation. I had my doubts they would investigate my concerns any further. I sought clarity as I journaled, talked with trusted friends, and silently contemplated my next step.

Before I knew it, I was boarding a plane in Minneapolis, with a destination of Monrovia. I had concluded that I was not in Liberia for the U.S. government or Samuel K. Doe. I was there for my students, who were counting on me to teach them agriculture and science and help them study to pass the national exam. I loved my students, and some of them had great potential. One of them, Julia, was about to become the second girl to graduate from Barclayville High School; her sister was the first a couple of years earlier. How could I not be there to help her achieve her goal?

I returned to Barclayville and was happy to find that my colleagues had been released from jail. I celebrated with Julia on her graduation day and I completed my second year, never having a moment's regret.

My heart never left the people of Liberia, who suffered the consequences of war. During my Christmas break back home, I had a choice of which home I wanted at that moment . . . I chose Liberia.

Kelley Jewett was a Peace Corps volunteer high school agricultural instructor in Barclayville, Liberia, from 1985 to 1986. She completed her medical training in the U.S. and returned to Liberia during the civil war in 1991 as the medical director of the Church World Service medical relief team in Monrovia. Kelley returned again from 1999 to 2002 with the United Methodist Church as a physician at Ganta Hospital. She currently practices family medicine in St. Paul, Minnesota, specializing in immigrant and refugee medicine.

ESCAPING LIBERIA, PART I: MY FIRST FOURTEEN HOURS

WILLIAM BODUO'S STORY AS TOLD TO AND WRITTEN BY TERRI ENRIGHT

In 2008, when I met William Boduo, an immigrant from Liberia, I was immediately drawn into his incredible tale of triumph over tragedy. I vowed to share his inspirational account, which is actually the story of tens of thousands of Liberians. Though this tale of deadly escape during Liberia's civil war is rarely documented, it should never be forgotten. This is William Boduo's story:

Today is the day we all feared. I remember September 9, 1990, as if it were yesterday. Liberia's situation went from alarming to critical in a moment's time. Samuel Doe was lured out of the capital, brutally tortured and killed by guerilla leader, Prince Johnson. This was especially troublesome to us because Doe was, as I am, of the Krahn ethnic group. His mother and my grandmother grew up in the same village of Zia Town. He was the first indigenous president in Liberia's history. As Doe began building up our country, we had high hopes, but in the end, he was just like all of our past leaders, misusing funds for self-gain and mercilessly exerting oppressive power against his opposition.

Two groups, one led by Prince Johnson and another by Charles Taylor, retaliated against Doe, starting a thirteen-year civil war in 1989. Taylor's rebels vowed to exterminate all members of Doe's Krahn ethnic group with their vicious chant "No Krahn will live!" This left us quaking in fear. We heard reports that Taylor's rebels were marching up the main road from the capital, terrorizing every village and indiscriminately killing men, women, and children. My own three-year-old half-brother was taken from his home and never seen again. My other brother survived being shot. A little girl told me her Krahn grandfather was skinned alive. Escaping to the Ivory Coast was our only option, even though this was the rainy season and travel was almost impossible.

We left our home, the only life we knew, at 5 a.m. In a torrential downpour and under the security of darkness, we fled with just the clothes on our backs, a small bit of food, and our memories. I left everything behind: my secure life as a pastor, as an elder of nine churches, and as a schoolteacher. I told myself, "Don't look back, put one foot in front of the other. Keep going and get away. Belongings are nothing compared to the safety of your family." If you had to walk away from everything with death threatening your family, I ask you, what would you take? Draining all my strength was the weight of my precious three-year-old son wrapped in a *lappa* on my back and my six-year-old daughter on my shoulder. A sack of rice balanced in another cloth around my neck. My pregnant twenty-two-year-old wife, Beatrice, was not able to carry anything. Concern for this new baby was always on our minds.

Fear of the rebels kept us moving forward hour after long hour. As the sun came up, we were joined by hundreds of others trudging beside us, blank stares of the hungry and frightened. Old people who couldn't walk were carried in makeshift hammocks. No cars could drive through this mud, so if you couldn't walk, you didn't make it. Beatrice saw a paralyzed old woman she knew who could only crawl. Carrying her through the deep mud became impossible, and after hours of effort, her family tearfully left her by the road in the muck. Later we heard that she had died there while people walked by. It was a time of great hardship, fear, and sorrow. People could only save themselves.

Our nightmare continued late into the evening. With almost two hundred pounds of weight on me, I was bone-tired. Just when I didn't think I could take another step, we arrived at the crossing camp on the bank of the Cavalla River bordering the Ivory Coast. Hundreds of other refugees were milling around, waiting their turn to be ferried across this raging river. Famished, I found a farmer selling rice and corn and was relieved to finally sit down and share some food with my family. As we wandered around looking for a spot to sleep for the night, we rejoiced at finding other friends and family who had made it. We shared stories of our miraculous escape. Amidst physical anguish and seemingly insurmountable hardships, we had found unknown reserves of courage and resilience deep within ourselves.

I wish I could tell you this was the end of my story, but it was not. As the eldest son, it was my responsibility to go back to Zia Town to find and rescue my mother and grandmother. In a heartrending departure, I left my pregnant wife and two small children there in the field, in the rain. Much later, I heard that friends helped them into the refugee camp, where they were safe. I could not predict their future, nor did I know the dangers I would soon face in the search for my mother and grandmother. My story had not yet ended.

Parents carrying children through the deep mud
Photo courtesy of EPA-EFE/Ahmed Jallanzo

ESCAPING LIBERIA, PART II: FAITH PROPELLED ME

At the beginning of the Liberian Civil War, after fleeing from Charles Taylor's rebel army with his wife and children to the Ivory Coast, William Boduo confronts new dangers in the effort to find and rescue his mother and grandmother. This is William Boduo's story:

With a few hours of restless sleep, I awoke to a light, cold drizzle of rain. Smells of cassava roasting over smoky fires filled my nostrils and hunger pangs tore at my empty stomach. My head was in a fog and my body ached from yesterday's fourteen-hour arduous walk in deep mud with my two small children and my pregnant wife. My mind reeled as I recalled our narrow escape from the killing spree of Taylor's advancing rebel army. By the river, waves of people were jammed into congested queues waiting to cross. A compassionate Krahn family agreed to take my pregnant wife and two children into their home until it was safe for them to cross.

Relieved that they were cared for, my thoughts turned to the fate of my mother and grandmother, who lived in Zia Town. As the eldest son and head of the family, I was responsible for securing their safety. To rescue them, I would have to make the long, difficult trek back to Zwedru through the rebel territory I had just left. With only the shirt on my back, I pushed against the great tide of people advancing toward the border. I will never forget the horrific scenes I encountered on the return journey: the smell and sight of corpses of old people who had died in the mud left by families too exhausted to carry them; a woman giving birth by the side of the filthy road; mud-soaked children crying out from hunger and fatigue, clutching to the pant legs of exhausted parents.

A ghost town greeted me back in Zwedru. Everything had been abandoned. Looters were everywhere, ransacking houses. Tired and dazed, I found a truck going in my direction to Zia Town. After a sleepless night's travel, we discovered the village blocked by trigger-happy soldiers, one of the last regiments of our murdered President Doe.

Gunmen lurked in the perimeters. Suspicious men arrested me, stripped me down to my briefs, and interrogated me in a dark, damp cell for hours without food or water. Memories of people being dragged from their homes and shot in the street plagued my mind. Bravery seeped away. But this was not my day to die. God, in His mercy, sent me a protector in the form of an interrogator who knew me when I was a high-ranking officer in the ROTC. The other soldiers were so impressed by his stories of my reputation that they released me with profound apologies and a bowl of rice.

In the end, when I found my grandmother, she refused to flee with me, believing she was too old and a burden. She believed Doe's army was there to protect his home village and that she would be safe. On the contrary, Zia Town had become a target and one of the worst places to be during the war. One year later, in 1991, Doe's army ran out of food and ransacked all the homes. They forced the residents by gunpoint to carry food to their camp. My grandmother, who could hardly walk, was unable to help. The rebels shot her and left her body to be trampled in the roadside mud. It is still hard to forgive myself for not insisting she come with me.

I continued my search for my mother and her husband, following various rumors of their whereabouts. Traipsing from village to village through tangled jungle paths, I finally found them hidden in a secluded mud hut. I convinced them they had to flee.

After many long, grueling days of hiking and sleeping in the cold mud with no fire or food, we made it to the border with only the Cavalla River between us and freedom. Dread of drowning overwhelmed us as we crossed on a makeshift boat of planks and metal drums. Danger turned to triumph as we stepped our feet on solid ground in the Ivory Coast. Weeks of peril were finally over. I felt an overwhelming sense of gratitude when people welcomed us with food, shelter, and protection. In the months ahead, I got established as a refugee and was then free to travel to reunite with my family. Mixed emotions flooded my heart: relief that we were all finally safe, sadness that everything of my previous life was gone, trepidation at the unknown in front of me. The only thing I knew for sure was that God would continue to be my provider.

Faith propelled me for thirteen more years as my family and I moved from place-to-place as refugees eking out a living. This faith was exactly what I needed one frightful morning in 2003 when I suddenly woke to the distressing cry, "Wake up! Wake up! Quickly! You must flee and go into hiding!" Taylor-backed rebels attempted to massacre us in our new home in Abidjan, Ivory Coast. We barely escaped with our lives.

Now with our family of six children, we crammed into a car and once again fled to another refugee camp in Accra, Ghana. Tent after tent lined the camp. There was no food. Theft was rampant. Then, at the height of our desperation, we learned that the United States was opening refugee applications. I joined tens of thousands of others also desperate to enter into the U.S. Embassy to apply. The army could not control the chaos, and the hearings were going to be canceled. Suddenly, I felt empowered by the Holy Spirit to take bold action. I took the microphone and spoke to my people about a future of peace—an end to war. The commanding officer was so grateful I had prevented a riot, that he immediately led me into the embassy to be the first one to register to come to America. We felt like we had won the million-dollar lottery.

William Bodou in the U.S., 2015

That is how my family and I landed in the United States in 2004, where we now had the opportunity to realize our dreams, educate our children, and live in peace and security. We knew there would be new challenges to overcome, but we had faith that God would give us the courage to create a new beginning.

In 2012, the International Criminal Court in The Hague charged and convicted Charles Taylor of war crimes committed against civilians in neighboring Sierra Leone and sentenced him to fifty years in prison. He has never been convicted of war crimes in Liberia.

President Samuel Doe, who was killed and never convicted, also committed war crimes in Liberia that the world will not forget.

Terri E. Enright, a pediatric occupational therapist, is the director of ESORM Africa, a nonprofit she co-founded that supports three schools in Liberia. Terri and her Liberian partner, Rev. William Boduo, travel to Liberia frequently to support Liberian pastors, teachers, and students through education. Over one hundred orphans receive a free education and daily lunch through ESORM's child sponsorship program.

Rev. William Younsia Boduo, born in Zwedru, Liberia, fled to the Ivory Coast during the civil war, where he pastored several churches and taught school in the refugee camps. Under threat of his life, he relocated his family to the U.S. in 2004. He and Terri Enright founded a nonprofit, ESORM Africa, in 2009 that promotes education in Liberia. Visit www.Esorm.com.

THE OTHER SIDE

BY KAREN E. LANGE

It was November 2004 and I was returning from Liberia to the United States. At the time, with the country just a year out from the "second" civil war, you could not fly direct from Monrovia to Europe. It was necessary to lay over in Ghana. And I was happy, because it would allow me to see my friends' four children, stuck here since 2003, when, with rebels approaching, they had left the Liberian capital.

I set out early that Sunday from the airport hotel in Accra, on my way to the Buduburam Refugee Camp. I was trying to make it back by brunch from the camp—a little city on the outskirts of the Ghanaian capital filled with Liberians who had fled their country's civil war.

As the taxi carried me up the main road along the coast, I tried to glimpse the beaches and resorts that drew tourists to Ghana. A couple of weeks before, while visiting Liberia to do a story on the country's forest, I had spent a nervous day under curfew in Monrovia, sheltering in the house of some fellow returned Peace Corps volunteers on Mamba Point, while riots between Christians and Muslims spread from Red Light on the city's outskirts into downtown. Smoke rose from churches and mosques. Looking down from the heights, I could see bands of looters. Fighters from rebel factions were supposed to have turned in their guns during the previous months. But people wondered if they might just be waiting to dig up caches of weapons. In Ghana, people wondered if there might be fighters among the refugees.

"Buduburam," the taxi driver said. "Why do you want to go there?"

"To see my friends' children. They ran from Liberia. Their parents are in the United States, but they can't get visas."

From 1984 to 1986, the children's father, Jesse, had been my Peace Corps counterpart in Zota District, Bong County. We worked together as extension aides, teaching farmers to grow fresh-water fish in ponds. He was my interpreter—of the local Kpelle language, of culture, of the dark politics of the mid-1980s—and my guide along rough dirt roads and bush paths that led to villages and farms. In 1994, during the first civil war, I saw him briefly in Danane, Cote d'Ivoire, where Liberians took refuge. In 1997, I met his growing family when I passed through Zota District as a Friends of Liberia elections observer. Then I got an email: His wife, Keabeh, had won the Diversity Lottery. With my husband and I as sponsors, Jesse and Keabeh came to America in 2000, leaving their four school-aged children with family members in Monrovia. They planned to send for the children as soon as they found jobs, a place to rent, and the money for plane tickets. They didn't realize it would take years to get visas.

"Buduburam is a bad place," the taxi driver said. "Criminals live there. They rob people."

I did not try to argue.

The taxi slowed. We were at the camp. An armored personnel carrier stood by the entrance. The plan was for the Liberians to go home now. The UN had offered to fly them back and give them four months' food and supplies like jerry cans and soap. But the refugees were not ready. They did not trust that the peace would hold.

I walked down the camp's main dirt street, past Liberian businesses grown there during years of exile to the house where the children were staying with their aunt who had brought them here overland from Monrovia. Jesse sent her money for the children, but he had come to suspect they saw little of it—she spent the money on her own kids.

I greeted the aunt, then asked to see the children. They were wearing their best clothes—slacks and button-up shirts and dresses—ready to go with me to eat at the hotel: fifteen-year-old Jesse Jr., thirteen-year-old Kollie, eleven-year-old Telema, and nine-year-old Korto. They called me "auntie." I took them into a windowless back room, out of the aunt's view, drew cash from my money belt, and pressed it into their hands.

"This is for you. Don't let her take it from you."

We found another taxi on the road and drove back to the hotel for the all-you-can-eat brunch. Jesse Jr., Kollie, Telema, and Korto were the only children in the restaurant. They moved self-consciously around the white-clothed dining room. The Ghanaian staff watched them, smiling encouragingly.

"Take what you want," I said, as we went up for food. "And you can go back and get more."

On the buffet table were scrambled eggs and bacon and sausage. Hard-boiled eggs. Oatmeal. Pancakes and syrup. Fruits—pineapple and guava and banana. Sliced bread and rolls and butter. Cereal and milk. And little cakes.

Quietly, the children loaded their plates, then sat with me at a long table. We talked about their new brother, Nukaama, who had been born in the United States. We talked about "the other side," as the U.S. is known in Kpelle. We talked about food. Korto liked the little cakes.

When I was sure they had eaten all they wanted, I hugged the children and found a taxi to take them back to Buduburam, away from the airport, away from the planes that flew daily toward their parents.

With several hours before I had to start my return journey to the United States via Europe, I sat by the hotel pool and slowly sipped a beer. I watched expats wade in the shallows and chat while holding drinks with their legs dangling in the deep end. The children, now on their way back to the camp guarded by armored personnel carriers, did not own bathing suits. But, again and again, I wished that they might be there, playing in the pool. The sight of the expats relaxing seemed obscene. Tears pooled in my eyes. My beer grew warm.

How strange this world that spanned so great a divide. How generous. How cruel. How miraculous that I, who once barely knew where Liberia was, now was bound to these children—powerless as I prepared to return to America alone.

In December 2005, Jesse Jr., Kollie, Telema, and Korto were reunited with their parents at Dulles International Airport outside Washington, D.C.

Karen E. Lange served as a Peace Corps volunteer in Belefanai from 1984 to 1986. After witnessing the rigged election and attempted coup of 1985, she became a journalist. She returned to Liberia as a journalist and also a Friends of Liberia elections observer. Her husband, Stuart Gagnon, traveled there with her during the war. Her two children hope to travel there someday.

MY RESILIENT "SON"

BY MARK ZELONIS

It hit me like a punch to the gut. An out-of-the-blue phone call in 1990 from a recently returned Peace Corps volunteer told me that our former houseboy, Gabriel, was in serious trouble. Liberia's new civil war was intensifying, and rebel forces led by Charles Taylor were seeking out opponents. Apparently, Gabriel was one of them. His life was in danger. We had to work fast.

Eighteen years before, Gabriel Mongrue, the houseboy for me and my housemate (and future wife) Sally, and a pupil in Sally's sixth-grade class had shared with us a tremendous amount of knowledge about the local culture. He looked out for us and introduced us to important people in our village of Karnplay: the blacksmith, the weaver and potter, and even the paramount chief. Without him, I would have missed out on much of the life in that distant corner of Liberia. I treasured all he taught me about the countryside, farms, and the local villagers I visited as a tree crops technician in the early 1970s.

After departing Liberia and the Peace Corps, we invested in Gabriel's future, supporting him financially to attend Saint Mary's High School in Sanniquellie, the Kakata Rural Teachers Institute, and later, the University of Liberia. He truly wished to be a leader in the country's future. I knew he had great potential with his maturity and genuine care for his fellow Liberians. The fact that he was now a marked man for those very traits sickened and terrified me.

I soon got word from him. He called while hiding under a desk at the Telecom building in Monrovia. I sensed some relief in his voice, but it was clear that time was of the essence. To avoid being captured, he slept under hospital beds or in boats offshore.

Mark with Gabriel and his mother, 1972

Working diplomatic channels in our home state of Rhode Island, Sally and I managed to send him a one-way business class ticket to the U.S. Then, we paid a clerk in Monrovia a dash of twenty-five dollars to obtain a passport. All seemed to be going to plan until the rebels destroyed the airport the day before Gabriel's departure. With another wire of money from us, he was able to get a short flight to Sierra Leone, where he found the airport closed. A local man invited him to his home for the night and got him back to the airport the next day to catch his flight to Amsterdam.

I had requested that Gabriel call us as soon as he arrived in Amsterdam, but he had only twenty-two Liberian cents in his pocket. A fellow traveler from India recognized his plight and offered him a Dutch guilder to make the call. Things were starting to go his way.

He finally made his connecting flight to the U.S. When I collected Gabriel at JFK, I found him greatly relieved but very thin. I hugged him for a long time, both of us shedding copious tears. It was what he showed me next that made me realize how close he had come to dying. From inside his tiny bag of meager belongings, he pulled a recent issue of the *Daily Observer.* On its cover was a horrific photo of two of his friends, brutally beheaded and left on a street by the same rebels who had searched for Gabriel.

Gabriel lived with us for nearly three years until he got on his feet in his new country. I have learned so much from him. I remember how naïve I was as a twenty-one-year old when I landed in Liberia in 1971 as a volunteer. Helping others to better themselves seemed a noble goal. My efforts to get local farmers to grow coffee and cacao as a cash crop were not as successful as I may have wished, but I made friends with incredible people like Gabriel, who helped me learn about the culture of Liberia and ease my transition.

I continue to admire Gabriel's tenacity and resilience. His new life in the U.S. has not been easy. He has faced adversity and discrimination at work. He has been denied promotions due to his lack of a green card. He has been sexually harassed by a college professor, and falsely accused of harassment by a young woman. I have personally witnessed him being followed by security in department stores and museums, simply because he did not meet the typical visitor profile.

But that didn't stop him. Gabriel worked for a decade as a certified nursing assistant in a Rhode Island veterans' home and has since served as a community living aide for citizens unable to care for themselves. He aims to retire soon and work with fellow Liberians to form a not-for-profit organization to work for free and fair elections, and to help Liberians back home fight corruption.

This kind-hearted, resourceful, and thoughtful man has become the son I never had. Though he was not able to accomplish his goals back home, here, he has influenced many through his compassionate and gentle nature.

Mark Zelonis was a Peace Corps volunteer in Karnplay, Nimba County, from 1971 to 1972. As a tree crops technician, he assisted local farmers in growing coffee and cacao. He later earned a master's degree in public horticulture administration and has overseen the operations of several public gardens. Now retired, he leads tours to gardens and cultural sites around the country.

MY HEART SINGS

BY JOAN SAFRAN HAMILTON, PHD

July 19, 1997, Election Day in Liberia, begins in the relatively cool dawn of another sweltering day in West Africa. I'm in Liberia with James Bowman as members of an election observers team from Friends of Liberia. A three-week commitment was required to determine if the registration and voting process of Liberia's first free election would be transparent and open. It is a way I can give back to the country that taught me so much when I served as a Peace Corps volunteer in 1965.

Seven years of brutal civil war killed more than two hundred thousand Liberians and left two-thirds of the remaining population displaced and living in unbelievable squalor. Everywhere, there is evidence of war from the burned-out carcasses of vehicles, eight-foot-high piles of garbage, and mounds of crumbled buildings. Mold grows everywhere. Nothing seems whole or untouched. If I let myself cry, the tears may never stop.

A fragile peace is being maintained by the thirteen thousand soldiers who make up a UN/African peacekeeping force. Their rifles, machine guns, and checkpoints seem to be everywhere. Times are so uncertain that the election featuring thirteen presidential candidates, including several warlords, has already been postponed once. The populace is exhausted from the horrors they've witnessed and the constant threat of renewed conflict.

James and I arrive in Kakata, the headquarters for a large peacekeeping contingent whose commander makes sure we have an escape plan in case fighting breaks out. Liberia saw intense fighting, including the atrocities of beheadings committed by drugged child-soldiers. Despite my trepidation, I have faith that I'm meant to be here, whatever the outcome. At the same time, my fingers often touch the angel pin given to me by a co-worker at home "to keep me safe."

For brief moments I feel joy being back in Liberia like I'm twenty-two again. The smells of wood fires and palm oil, the thatched huts and colorful *lappas* are all so familiar. Even the dark nights lit mostly by kerosene lanterns remind me of the pre-electric era of my Peace Corps' days decades ago. Yet, an acute awareness of the recent violence and an atmosphere of fear hangs over me and Liberia. I've been in-country over a week and have yet to get a good night's sleep.

At 6:30 a.m., James and I arrive at Polling Site 0017, an empty school assembly hall filled with two rickety tables, four chairs, and a couple of cardboard voting booths. We find a long line of one hundred and fifty to two hundred silent voters, some waiting patiently since midnight for the polls to open at seven. We go inside, introduce ourselves, and take our places with two Liberian observers and two heavily armed soldiers. The presiding officer is a woman about forty years old. When she determines all is ready, she turns to those of us inside the hall and announces, "And now we will pray." The eight of us join hands to form a circle. I hold the wrist of one soldier. He holds his AK-47. An echo of "amen" follows her simple blessing for the election and a plea for peace.

The soldier whose wrist I held, goes outside, raises his rifle, and shouts, "And now we will all pray. One Christian and one Muslim. You must find among you someone to pray for us."

The long line is at first silent. In it are members of warring factions, displaced persons, and former combatants. Then, a man about a third of the way down the line speaks up,

"I will pray." His prayer is an echo of the prayer inside.

When he finishes, the soldier raises his gun again and shouts, "Now a Muslim!"

This time the silence lasts longer until a stately Mandingo in a flowing robe at the end of the line raises his hand, and he, too, prays out loud. I'm sure it's a prayer for peace.

The soldier puts down his gun, brings an empty ballot box out to show people, raises a clear plastic tub over his head and shouts. "Empty! You see that it is empty!"

He seals the box with a lock and picks up his rifle. Now we're ready to begin voting. The first man in line silently drops his ballot into the box. Applause erupts in the building and flows out the door and down the long line of voters like a row of falling dominoes.

There seems to be so much hope in the school assembly hall that I can smell it. I've spent days talking to people, observing, and taking notes. My part in the election process is complete. The longing for peace is so palpable that I feel myself relaxing for the first time since arriving back in Liberia.

Two days later, in the capital of Monrovia, the ballots have been counted. Waiting for the results of the election to be announced at an international press conference, I stand with my back against the wall in a crowded assembly hall at St. Theresa's school. Every square inch of the large classroom is occupied, including the open windows packed with spectators who can't manage to squeeze into the building.

At the front of the room, along with Liberian officials, are representatives from international organizations providing election observers: United Nations, European Union, African Union, and the Carter Center. Jimmy Carter, former U.S. President, is on the platform to personally present his group's findings. FOL is not yet ready to present its conclusions, however, the international representatives feel the urgency to do so. The whole country is holding its breath to hear who won and if the election was free and transparent. Most voted for Charles Taylor, the warlord who started the civil war and whose soldiers were responsible for countless atrocities. Voters claimed, "He broke it, let him fix it." or "If he loses, he will start the war again." If so, it could end the uneasy ceasefire being maintained by UN and African peacekeepers.

Television crews and reporters from around the world adjust their cameras. The room fills with subdued excitement as we wait for the proceedings to begin. There's a sense of expectancy but no real mystery. The outcome of the election seems a foregone conclusion—Charles Taylor will win because of his superior military power and financial resources. But, was the election won fairly? I watch and listen, eager to hear the official election announcement as history is made.

The hot, crowded room is full of sweaty bodies pressed wall-to-wall. I feel the perspiration dripping off the nape of my neck and my bangs are plastered to my forehead. I shift my weight from one leg to the other hoping we'll start soon. I'm wedged next to a Liberian man who appears to be in his mid-forties. I smile and ask about his connection to the election.

"I am with one of Monrovia's newspapers. Why are you here?"

He looks at the dog tags hanging around my neck, I explain, "I'm an observer with Friends of Liberia." He frowns, and I go on to say, "It's a group of mostly former Peace Corps volunteers."

His eyes light up and his face breaks into a huge grin. "Peace Corps! You were our *ma's* and our *pa's!* You taught us how to read and write. You taught us how to think. Unless Peace Corps says it is so, Liberians will not believe." He shakes my hand vigorously.

Just then, the press conference begins. I hear the introduction of dignitaries, but the words of a Liberian stranger drown out those spoken on stage. His words bring unexpected joy and tears to my eyes. I'm overcome by the gratitude in his voice and the warmth of his handshake. My heart sings.

The election was declared free and transparent with Charles Ghankay Taylor winning seventy-five percent of the vote.

Joan Safran Hamilton was an elementary school teacher in Voinjama and Vezala from 1965 to 1967. After the Peace Corps, she earned a PhD in Infant Development and worked for years in early intervention/early childhood special education. In 1997, she was an election observer and subsequently returned to Liberia with the FOL as a teacher trainer for five years with the Liberian Education Assistance Program (LEAP).

LETTERS NEVER WRITTEN

BY JOHN KUCIJ

In July of 1997, I traveled with a Friends of Liberia delegation to observe the national presidential election that was supposed to end the country's civil war. My wife, Lyn, and I had served as junior and senior high school teachers in Liberia in the early 1970s and had returned once with our young children in 1987 for a three-week visit. I wasn't prepared to see and hear what I did during those ten days a decade later. I saw senseless destruction. I learned of former students who had perished during the conflict. I met so many traumatized civilians.

Upon my return, my wife gave me several college-note blue books. She had filled the pages with diary entries while I was away and out of communication (during the pre-cell phone era). It was only then that I began to process the trip and wrote this poem:

letters never written until I was home with you
and the red dust, the stench of waterside market
and the smell of death at Spriggs Payne Airport
still clung to my being

letters never written while my butt ached from
deeply rutted roads and my head swelled with
reunions, lost Loma words, Johnny Walker Black
and child soldiers with zombie faces

letters never written to tell of missing limbs
and mangled lives and how old friends crouched
in the jungle quiet and still for days
eating insects and drinking rainwater from leaves
what can be said about
sewage ditches clogged with bleached human bones,
scores of abandoned burned-out vehicles
lining so many roads like the carcasses of buffalo,
entire neighborhoods collapsed piles of scrap tin and cinder?

almost too full to capture it all and unable to share
without tearing up day after exhausting day
it beat me up more than I could admit
to anyone but you

when I was most fragile I wrote letters in my heart
and reread them each evening
some for you some for our sons
some for our dear, loving friends

and I read them again when you showed me
your diary of my days away and I was able
to visit the you I had missed so much and the you
who missed me too and trusted me enough to go

John Kucij was a Peace Corps teacher at Voinjama High School, Liberia, from January 1971 until June 1973. He has a master's degree in human services administration and retired from Hudson Valley Community College, where he was director of the college's Workforce Development Institute. He and his wife, Lyn, remain actively involved with health and education projects in Liberia.

THE PHOTOGRAPH

BY MIKE WAITE

In 1997, I returned to my Peace Corps country of Liberia to serve as an election observer. After seven cruel years of war, there was a temporary peace and an election that everyone hoped would end the war, which had changed everything in Liberia.

I carried a photograph taken in 1975 by my wife, Mary Lynn, when I was a twenty-five-year-old Peace Corps forester. I looked really young, with wire-rimmed glasses, auburn hair, and a red beard in the picture. I was sitting by an older man with a pipe, Joe Kepue, a co-worker who always had a wide, missing-tooth smile. I liked that Joe stayed close to his Liberian roots, never trying to act more Western as others I worked with often did.

Mike with Joe Kepue, 1975

Joe could not read or write, yet he knew the bush better than any of us working in forestry. His job was as a tree finder. He already knew all the names of the trees in his native Gio language and had taught himself the common English and scientific names as well. With Joe on the back of my Suzuki 125 motorcycle, we traveled all around Nimba County. Together, we worked in the bush, visiting many small villages, where I gained a better understanding of rural Liberian life.

I had not seen Joe in twenty-two years. I hoped the photo would help me find him. However, after so many years, I knew the odds were slim. He could have died or more likely been displaced during the war, like so many others.

My election observer assignment was in Tappita, Nimba County, my former Peace Corps village. While there, I took time to look for my old Peace Corps house. Although everything was totally different in 1997, I found that the house was still standing.

While investigating the changes, I met an old man who wondered if I was a volunteer whom he remembered from years past. I took out my photo to show him how I had looked those many years ago. The old man did not know me, but he recognized Joe, and told me he lived in a village about fifteen miles away.

Two days later, I reunited with my old friend. We shook hands, embraced, and examined each other. Joe was sixty-two, and unlike me, he looked much the same. I was clean-shaven, no longer wore glasses, and had entirely gray hair. We traveled to his home, where we recounted the events of our time working together.

Twenty-two years gave us, if not wisdom, at least, perspective. I have seen friendships blossom and wither and know the importance of keeping and sustaining a good friend. Joe had seen and survived the horrors of a war that touched even the most remote villages. We knew our time together was short and precious. Our differences made long, lively discussions difficult, but it was not important. When the pauses became too long, we knew it was time for a walk. I will never forget Joe's words when I asked him what it was like to lose everything he owned. His reply was simple and direct.

"We have our lives. That is what is important."

Joe treated me to palm wine and pepper soup and gave me several chickens. Before leaving, I gave Joe clothing and money and paid several of his grandchildren's school tuitions.

The election observation trip was a powerful experience. I bounced on Liberia's bumpy, unmaintained roads, found my former house, and worked with remarkable people to observe and monitor the 1997 elections. I witnessed Liberians getting up at four-thirty in the morning to walk, some for many miles, and get in long lines to vote. For many, it was the first time. Finding my old friend Joe made the journey emotionally overwhelming.

In 2009, twelve years after my election monitoring trip, I again visited Liberia. After working on an environmental project, I traveled to Tappita, where I heard Joe now lived. In 1999, two years after the election of Charles Taylor, a second civil war had begun. Throughout the fighting, northeastern Liberia, including Nimba County, was hit especially hard. I walked to a house scarred with bullet holes and burn marks and shouted, "Joe Kepue." A blind, frail man walked out of a room with a look of astonishment. With a wide smile, he replied, "Mr. Mike," as we both moved toward each other for a big hug. No longer able to see, Joe's two daughters took care of him in the small room where he spent most of his time.

Later that day, we shared palm butter and pepper soup and told the same old stories of our time thirty-four years earlier. I bought rice and other goods and left money for the family, promising to stop by a few days later on a return trip.

My return visit was short. We all knew this would be the last time Joe and I would be together. Teary-eyed, we had a long embrace and said our final goodbyes. I carried a chicken and my memories to a waiting taxi and rode down the dusty road to Monrovia.

Three months later, a Liberian number showed up on my caller ID. I answered. The voice on the other end informed me that my friend, Joe Kepue the tree finder, had passed away.

Mike Waite served as a Peace Corps volunteer in Tappita, Nimba County, from 1974 to 1975, working as a forester. He managed the Friends of Liberia website from 2002 to 2011 and made return trips to Liberia in 1997, 2004, and 2009. Retired, Mike travels frequently and enjoys spending time with his wife, children, and grandchildren.

THE BICYCLE

BY PAT REILLY

Buchanan was not an idyllic Peace Corps posting. Not that the typical volunteer's posting was necessarily picturesque, but this gritty, ore mining town, the second largest city in Liberia, was far from my imagined village setting with respectful neighbors and thatch-roofed schoolrooms. Its redeeming characteristics were that it fronted on the Atlantic Ocean, albeit tinted orange by the detritus of ore processing, and that it had coal tar roads.

Early in my service in 1973, a friend sent fifty dollars to spend on something that made my life easier. That was a quarter of my monthly big city salary, so it was a big deal. With it, I went to one of the many Lebanese-owned shops and bought a Chinese-made blue bicycle to get around on. It was a simple affair—no gears, just brakes, a bell, and fat tires—but it got me to school on time, to the bathing beach on weekends, and to the grocery store at the mining company when I was feeling flush with all the taxi money I had saved.

The bicycle also stoked the envy of every boy in my Vai Town neighborhood, and it would be stolen more than once. It was so distinctive that it was always found and returned by my zealous students for a reward. When I was "coming to go" in local parlance, it broke my heart to leave "Bluebell" behind. There were many contenders for this prize. I conferred it on the youngest son of a fellow teacher. He was a bright, quiet, promising six-year-old who could barely reach the pedals. I sensed he would treasure it.

Little did any of us know what lay ahead for Liberia in the next three decades. As the nation descended into civil war and economic deprivation in the late 1980s, former volunteers formed Friends of Liberia (FOL) to do whatever we could to help the people with whom we had lived. FOL advocated for U.S. support for Liberia on Capitol Hill, sent a pediatrician to JFK Hospital in Monrovia, hosted a number of visiting Liberian delegations and testified before Congress on the rampant atrocities we learned about from friends and former students. We mediated among warring parties. We observed an election, and we distributed a news bulletin that kept even some at the State Department, which had pulled out of Liberia in 1990, informed about developments on the ground.

As we sent money for the rebuilding of an elementary school, I wondered what was happening in those classrooms. I began to imagine improving education with the wealth of teachers in our former volunteer ranks. In 1998, when many thought the brutal eight-year war was over, I proposed a project that would bring back former volunteer master teachers to pass on their skills to Liberian teachers, who had not had professional development in more than a decade. A generous foundation sent two FOL college deans and me to Liberia to assess what the teachers there needed and wanted.

Walking into Liberian classrooms for the first time in twenty-five years, we saw and heard that they needed everything, especially trained teachers. We succeeded in getting funds and found three wonderful volunteer teachers to go with me the following summer for the first workshop of what would become LEAP (the Liberian Education Assistance Project) and would continue with annual trainings for thirteen years.

My first return to post-war Liberia earlier in 1998 before the other FOL fact-finders arrived, traveling alone, was traumatic for me. I had to fly in through another African country, change planes, suffer delays, land after midnight in Robertsfield, where I was fleeced by customs officials, and exit into a melee that made the Buchanan taxi stand look like a Sunday school picnic. There was no luggage belt, just a mountainous pile of every box and bag from the plane and a scrum of men pushing to claim them. The combatants were not only the people who owned the bags, but the taxi drivers who wanted business and so claimed luggage and therefore the owner. That, and the experience of seeing the effects of the war on familiar terrain, had me crying for the forty-five minute trip into Monrovia.

Months later, when I returned with three '60s-era volunteer master teachers and sixteen bags of materials for the first workshop, I wanted to spare the teachers the baggage claim experience. I left them to argue their way past customs while I breezed through because of my recent passport stamp. We had a van waiting outside but the suitcase gauntlet to run in between. Braced for a sixteen-round fight, I pulled only one bag from the heap and despaired of not getting them all. Just then, a uniformed police officer offered his help. Now my guard was really up. In Buchanan, the police were always on the take. How much would it cost to get a policeman's help with all those bags? Exhausted and bathed in sweat, I agreed to point while he used his uniformed authority and wiry muscles to grab each item. Then, with feigned hysteria, I guarded the stuff from taxi drivers. On it went for fifteen more bags. My relief at retrieving all the materials was overwhelming. I pushed a wad of U.S. bills at his hand, but he waved me away. In the heat and the dust, I thought I was hallucinating.

"You gave me the bike," he said, smiling.

I looked at the man's sad-eyed, preternaturally weathered features, and then I recognized his face: it was the little guy who had reached for the pedals all those years before. His next words brought me to tears.

"I'm sorry," he said with genuine contrition, "I lost the bike in the war."

Pat Reilly was a Peace Corps English teacher in Buchanan from 1972 to 1974. A longtime Friends of Liberia board member, she served as president, communications and development director, and started the Liberian Education Assistance Project. She chaired the National Peace Corps Association board. She was a newspaper editor for twenty years and a spokesperson for two U.S. agencies. She lives in Marshall, Virginia.

The Beyond War Award
honors you
Susan Greisen
for your efforts
through the Peace Corps
to build
a world beyond war.
December 6, 1987

BEYOND WAR

BY SUSAN E. GREISEN

I. NEBRASKA

I learned about war in high school.
The Civil War.
World War I.
World War II.
The Korean War.
Bombs and bullets were America's power.

But Vietnam?
Walter Cronkite on the 6 p.m. news
Taught me everything I knew.
I learned about it from my family, too.

The draft loomed over all the boys.
My brother? Deferred. A football injury.
My cousin? He returned from 'Nam
With both legs blown off above the knee.

Me? Young. Naïve. Isolated.
On the farm in Nebraska,
I knew no more than that.

But still,
Despite my sheltered life,
I wanted to help.
To serve.

II. ZORGOWEE

A TV commercial
Delivered the message
I wanted to hear:
"The toughest job you'll ever love.
Join the Peace Corps."

Just nineteen.
My only credentials:
Farm smarts and
A practical nurse's license.
What would I do?
A health educator, I said,
"My way to help. To serve.
In Zorgowee, Liberia."

No simple mission in 1971.
Challenges and barriers abounded.
Few medications, few resources,
Poverty aplenty.
Pregnant women,
Infants and children
Suffered most.

No bombs or bullets in Zorgowee back then.
But still, there was plenty of death.
High morbidity and high mortality
From preventable illnesses:
Malnutrition,
Malaria,
Diarrhea.
They were killers, too.

What weapons could I use?
Humane weapons:
Acceptance,
Respect,
Education.
That was my job. My mission.

My only teaching aids,
A felt board made from a baby blanket,
Cardboard cutouts and tape,
These, too, were my weapons
Against disease.

Villagers listened,
Soon, they understood.
Clinic attendance for
Prenatal exams,
Infant vaccinations,
And education soared.
International visitors asked,
"What's the secret of your success?"
"Building relationships," I said.
"Building trust."
"These are my tools."
That was my answer.

On every job I've worked since then
I've sent a silent thank you
To my people in Zorgowee.
They taught me
How to strive
To stay alive
And not give up.
They never gave up on me.
I never gave up on them.

Then the bullets came.
For two decades.
Two brutal civil wars
Ravaged Liberia.
Stories tell
Of the destructive scars
The wars left behind.
But Liberians remember
Those of us who served
In times of peace,
. . . before the bullets.
They still hold us close
In their hearts.
And so do we.
A bridge of human connection.
An everlasting bond.

III. THE WORLD

Today we have new wars to fight
The wars of pandemics and epidemics
Ebola
HIV/AIDS
SARS
COVID . . .
Enemies we need to fight.
Enemies we need to conquer.
United, we win.
Divided, we cannot.

A framed plaque,
Hangs in my home:
The Beyond War Award
Honors you,
Susan Greisen,
For your efforts
Through the Peace Corps
To build a world
Beyond war.

"Beyond War"
Reminds me daily
That America's power,
Is beyond
The bombs and bullets of destruction.
Her real power is
The strength of a resilient foundation.
Both at home and abroad.

A foundation of
Acceptance,
Respect,
Education,
This is a foundation
That endures.

Susan E. Greisen served in Peace Corps Liberia from 1971 to 1973, and Tonga, from 1973 to 1974, as a health education volunteer. She later worked as an RN public health specialist for CARE in Cameroon from 1980 to 1982. Susan was honored to lead the FOL project that published this anthology. Her award-winning memoir, *In Search of Pink Flamingos*, features her time in Liberia. Learn more at susangreisen.com.

PART III
REBUILDING HOPE
(THE LATTER YEARS)

THE RICHNESS OF LIFE

BY BARBARA J. BURKE

That day, the same screened doors sounded off with a signature hushed clap as patients entered Kolahun District Hospital's inpatient ward. Human life in all stages came through those doors. Front and center were two large, adjoining tables that served as both nursing station and triage area. These tables were the center of our universe, and our lives revolved around them.

In 2007, I joined The International Rescue Committee (IRC) team to serve as medical director at Kolahun Hospital. The once-thriving hospital was destroyed during the civil war. In 2004, Doctors Without Borders reopened the hospital, eventually transitioning hospital operations to the IRC upon my arrival. After two civil wars, health care in Liberia was largely unavailable, tentative at best.

We were a team of Liberians from Bong, Lofa, and Montserrado Counties, some returning from exile in Sierra Leone, Guinea, and Ivory Coast. We were Ghanaian, Australian, Sierra Leonian, and American. We teemed with life, even as those around us died. We laughed, yelled, and wore invisible shields of numbness in order to endure, while others worked with composure and grace.

In Kolahun's main hospital ward, nurses screamed patient names over the intermittent howl of the evening generator while dispensing antimalarials, antibiotics, and other drugs. I still hear Nurse Juliana's voice, "Fallah, Ibrahim, Theresa!" Mothers beckoned the call, tightening the wraps at their waists before grasping their children's upper arms. Infants and children screamed after injections.

Physician assistants and nurses directed the chaos into an organized flow. "You no small man!" Justin Kerwillain would say, hastening action from anyone who could hear him. "Come now, get the diazepam! Let's go! Let's go!" Toddlers with malaria and seizures required urgent intervention.

The afternoon's heat brought an influx of patients from Lukasu, Popalahun, Kamatahun, and Bolahun via the International Committee of the Red Cross (ICRC) vehicle: malnourished kids with big eyes, stunted children with edema, toddlers gasping for air, pale little ones suffering malaria-induced anemia. Miranda Odam was the accompanying ICRC nurse. Her rare, gentle manner and soothing Australian accent appeased even the most distressed patients.

Babies cried as fingers were pricked to test for malaria and anemia. Young children stoically obliged. Hammocks pushed through the screen doors with fat-bellied women, injured motorcyclists, snake-bite victims, and those who fell from palm trees. A wheelbarrow from the out-patient department delivered those who were seizing, gasping, or spasmodic due to tetanus. For the critically ill, everything that could be done was concomitantly executed: IV-insertion, type and screening for transfusion, and oxygenation (but only when there was fuel and a functioning generator to power the oxygen concentrator). Life's fragility was magnified when resources were contingent. Still, the richness of life pulsated with the delivery of each newborn, just as it wailed with every death.

Nurse aides circulated, recording temperatures and squirting acetaminophen into the mouths of febrile children. They doled out therapeutic feedings for the malnourished and oral rehydration solution for the dehydrated. Morale was tethered to our supplies. Low supplies, low morale. Pediatric anti-tuberculous formulations were difficult to access. Insulin was depleted. A small stock of rabies vaccine and rabies immunoglobulin was consumed after treatment of three rabid dog-bite victims. The fourth victim, a sixteen-year-old girl, suffered a rabid death. The world failed her.

The generator sputtered as the fuel ran low. A few portable, solar-powered lights went dark by 2:00 a.m.

As the rainy season progressed, the road from Gbarnga became muddier, and supplies dwindled further as the rain fell harder, drowning out our voices as it struck the corrugated zinc roof. Empty pharmacy shelves left us defenseless in the face of disease. Our universe became more isolated and lonelier. We rationed diazepam as a five-year-old succumbed to tetanus. A nineteen-year-old man with sickle-cell anemia died of acute chest syndrome—our meager narcotics worthless. The world failed him too.

I tried to process the losses and learn from the deaths by going through the "Why didn't I . . ."

"Why didn't I order more diazepam?"

"Why didn't I resuscitate that child?"

The majority of patients improved, a testament to the human body. For those patients who made it out those screened doors, there remained the question of what life would hold for them. Would the children attend school? Would parents tuck in their kids under mosquito nets? Would children complete their vaccinations?

The Peace Corps was not active in Liberia during 2007 to 2008, but in 2017, Peace Corps volunteers returned to Kolahun District. Volunteers like Ousman Sey, Carson Stacy, and Joni Burrell, all of whom were assigned to Kolahun District, to name a few. They not only taught in Kolahun District schools, they also developed programs to advocate for and provide adult education, empowerment for girls and women, improvement of literacy skills, advocacy for higher quality health care, and improved access to reproductive health education and resources for young adults. Brenna Blazis, a Peace Corps volunteer, evacuated during the COVID-19 pandemic in 2020, returned to Liberia on her own in 2021, and organized a community library in Kolahun. The efforts of Peace Corps volunteers in Liberia now reassure me that the patients who exit Kolahun's medical ward are stepping into a more encouraging future.

Since departing Kolahun in 2008, I have returned several times. Many of Kolahun's HIV patients have not survived, chiefly due to drug inaccessibility, particularly during West Africa's Ebola outbreak of 2014 to -2016, which claimed the lives of several members of Kolahun Hospital's staff. For the rest of us, Liberian nationals and expatriates alike, the richness of life steadfastly delivers wholesome fulfillment, in large part, because of access to health care and education.

Today, Kolahun Hospital continues to run low on pharmaceuticals and supplies. However, Dr. Andrew Cole's revolving drug program from the pre-war era has been reestablished through the contributions of Liberia's diaspora and others, including Dr. Bob Rufsvold and former PCV Saundra Williams. Thanks to Dr. David Okiror, there is now an operating room for C-sections. Bill Weaver and former PCV Shirley Halladay visited Kolahun in 2019, and due to their efforts, Kolahun Hospital was equipped with a solar-powered energy system in 2020. The lights stay on, the oxygen flows. The richness of Liberian life in Kolahun continues.

Barbara J. Burke worked with The International Rescue Committee as medical director of Kolahun District Hospital, Lofa County, from March 2007 to January 2008. Thereafter, she practiced emergency medicine at LBJ Tropical Medical Center, American Samoa, before departing for her seventh mission with Doctors Without Borders. Barbara regularly travels to Kolahun, serving as volunteer advisor to RESTORE HOPE: Liberia.

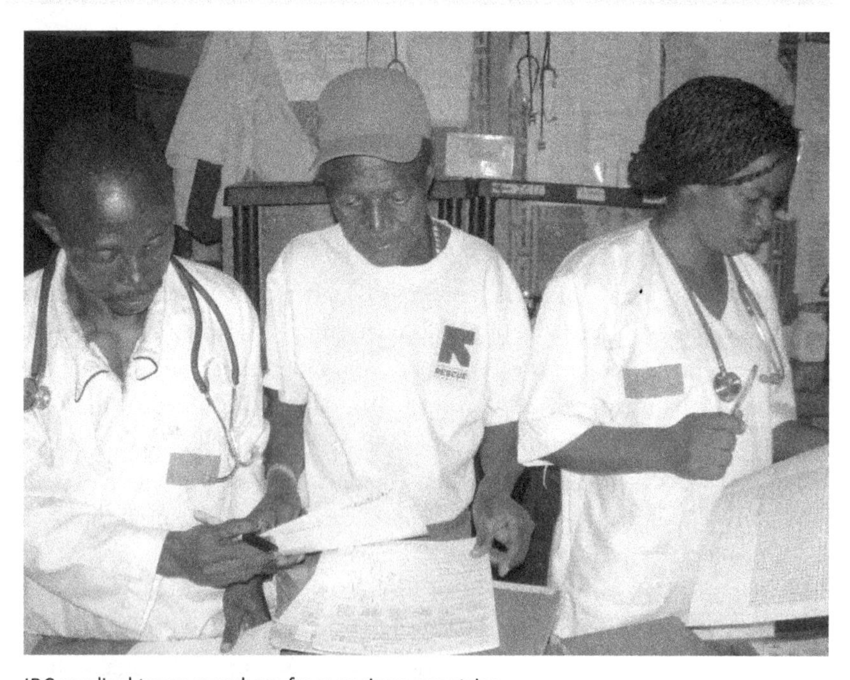

IRC medical team members from various countries

WOIWOR (WAY'-WAR)

BY JOHN KUCIJ

In December 2002, Woiwor came to live in Schenectady, New York. He was the twenty-six-year-old son of our language instructor from our Peace Corps days in Liberia in the early 1970s. He was born after we served, so we met him for the first time at John F. Kennedy Airport on a snowy day armed with gloves, a knit cap, and a winter jacket.

Woiwor was bright, industrious, and came legally as a winner of the Diversity Lottery. Around fifty thousand Liberians applied to immigrate to the United States. He was one of two hundred and fifty lucky souls chosen at random. Woiwor was "dry," a Liberian term for "thin," as time in the refugee camp meant poor nutrition. He survived a civil war while his oldest brother, a noncombatant, was executed. He survived a dangerous river crossing into Guinea, where he was able to teach French to fellow Liberians. Woiwor eventually reunited with his family and began the process of starting over. He came to America hungry—hungry to learn and to earn and to be an asset to the family he'd left behind.

Woiwor left behind over twenty siblings and a country where the economy and public infrastructure had been shattered by a senseless civil war during which rebel groups waged carnage on civilians nearly as much as on one another. If Woiwor could succeed, others might be able to follow.

His father had requested that we host him in our home "for a week or so" until he "got used to" America. Then, he would find a community of Liberians and move on with his life. We readily agreed but explained that it would need to be a longer visit, as there would be a lot of "getting used to." He lived with us for four months. His Liberian teaching credentials meant nothing in the U.S., so he got a job cleaning floors at our local hospital. Woiwor learned the bus routes and walked everywhere. The bitter cold quickly made Liberia's steamy, tropical rain forests a distant memory.

Years of war had driven his family out of the countryside and to the outskirts of the coastal capital of Monrovia. But Woiwor was a country boy at heart. He knew the ways of rural life and the many cultural traditions of his Loma tribe. He had grown up in a community with no paved roads, and only spotty access to clean water, electricity, and health care. Salaried jobs were rare, and most families were subsistence farmers.

Woiwor's rural community was large by Liberian standards and surrounded by dozens of villages connected to the world by a network of narrow footpaths winding through lush, tropical forests. Many students at the school where my wife and I taught walked miles roundtrip each day to attend. Our students and most of Woiwor's older siblings spent after-school hours at our home, asking numerous questions about life in America, picking up American English, and hoping to do small chores in return for various treats.

In Schenectady, Woiwor settled in nicely and was a joy to host. We told him stories of our early days in Liberia getting to know his family. Although he spoke good English, we enjoyed simple conversations in the Loma language his father had taught us. He was full of wonder and gratitude, but we knew all the changes were overwhelming for him. So much information to process. New tastes, new sounds, new smells, and new friends all vied for his attention. For all the informal education we could offer to ease his transition, there was much more we overlooked, presuming he understood. We missed much that baffled him.

The plentitude of America boggled his mind. His image of the U.S. emerged from occasional American-made action movies, from discarded English language magazines, and from the Western goods available from vendors in Monrovia's sprawling, crowded, open-air markets. He was like many immigrants who come to America and find the country much bigger, more diverse, more surprising and terrifying than they ever imagined. Here supermarkets have aisles devoted to pet food. Woiwor came from a place where every-day people struggled, sometimes fruitlessly, to find food.

After four months, Woiwor relocated to Niagara Falls, Ontario, where a half-brother and several cousins had lived for a few years. Six months after his arrival in North America, he moved in with a Liberian friend in Newark, New Jersey.

He worked several part-time jobs and pursued an undergraduate degree at Rutgers University. Woiwor earned a bachelor's in social work, obtained U.S. citizenship, and worked subbing in Newark schools. Eventually he earned a master's degree and started a family. He relocated to South Jersey, where he works at a state hospital as a counselor/social worker. Woiwor keeps in touch with our family and our friends who came to know him when he first arrived. He visits yearly with his wife and children, who are part of our own extended family.

His success is inspiring and not uncommon. Countless Liberians were caught in the middle of their civil wars. Those who fled with their lives to America brought their grit and courage as they searched for a way to better the situation for themselves and their families. They embody the qualities of an America that thrives on the foundation of diversity.

Peace Corps volunteers bring home more than memories, handicrafts, and great photos. They carry enduring relationships with people they came to know as close friends. Those bonds represent one of America's most powerful foreign policy tools.

John Kucij was a Peace Corps teacher at Voinjama High School, Liberia, from January 1971 until June 1973. He has a master's degree in human services administration and retired from Hudson Valley Community College, where he was director of the Workforce Development Institute. He and his wife, Lyn, remain actively involved with health and education projects in Liberia.

MET A PEACE CORPS, GAINED A SISTER

BY ELIZABETH V. SHERIFF

My life changed for the better in the year 1986 when I met a soft-spoken, kind-hearted, blonde-haired Peace Corps volunteer at the Old Maternity Hospital in Sinkor, Monrovia.

Liberia was among the various African countries where the Combating Childhood Communicable Diseases (CCCD) project operated. They were trying to find ways to reduce the high childhood mortality rate and improve the health situation of infants. It so happened that Sarai (my angel) was among the group of Peace Corps Liberia volunteers assigned to the program.

I remember when Sarai entered the room. She introduced herself to everyone, and we formed a bond instantaneously. From time to time, we got together when Sarai was in the city. She was not happy when she found out that my employment was temporary. Work was only available for me when information came into the CCCD from the health survey that my colleagues were doing in villages throughout Liberia.

Sarai mentioned that I was too ambitious and hardworking for a temp position, and she wished I had a permanent job. True to her hopes, Sarai came by my house one day waving the American Embassy newsletter "The Talking Drum." It included an ad for employment, and she encouraged me to apply.

For the first time in my life, I had to fill out a job application. Fortunately, I had started computer classes to improve my typing and technical skills. With the help of my instructor, I was able to complete my application. Then, I took it to the embassy, but, to my disappointment, the security guard at the gate would not allow me entrance into the compound. I went crying to Sarai, who took me to the embassy the next day, where I was tested and interviewed for the job.

Soon, I found myself employed in the most prestigious job of my lifetime. I started at the American Embassy as a temporary staff member. Due to my hard work, I was able to join the permanent staff. I worked at the embassy for ten years before I resigned to immigrate to the United States as a winner of the Diversity Visa lottery.

For thirty-five years, Sarai has been the best sister anyone could wish for in this world. Our relationship became more than friends when I got to the States. Ngor Sarai—as she became to me—left Liberia with the promise of coming back. During the Liberian civil war, she kept checking on me through the embassy telefax until I immigrated to the States and was safe.

Ngor Sarai and I stayed in touch throughout the years once I was in the States and had access to email and telephone calls. We got together every time she was on vacation in the States. On one of these occasions, she invited me, my husband, and our two boys for a memorable weekend in Washington, D.C. We stayed with her, went sightseeing, and watched the July 4th fireworks. I had seen fireworks before, but not at a close range. We drove from Virginia to D.C. and found a spot atop a bridge—along with a huge mass of other people. Ngor Sarai came well prepared with snacks and drinks for all. Watching the fireworks at close range was exciting and impressive, but also nerve-racking for me. I still jumped at every loud noise. They reminded me too much of the rockets and guns shooting during the war in Liberia. The boys had fun and cheered at every colorful spark that went up in the sky. They were unhappy when it ended, but I was relieved. I have never again watched fireworks at close range; I prefer to watch them on TV.

In 2006, Ngor Sarai first visited my home. I was overjoyed and could not believe it when she accepted my invitation. I wanted the whole world to know that I had a big, white sister who loved me enough to come to my home. My family and I planned a moonlight barbecue for her, inviting all the Liberian community that we knew. I wrote a speech telling everyone about my sister. We had a wonderful night with lots of Liberian food and drinks. Early the following morning, we went on a trip to Donnie

Amusement Park. On the bus ride there, I felt guilty that it might be too exhausting for Ngor Sarai, but to my surprise, she was stronger than me. She was the one walking and taking the boys on all the rides and games in the park. We even took a picture, which I cherish to this day.

Every time she drove through the New Jersey area, Ngor Sarai stopped for a visit—including the night of her seventieth birthday! I surprised her with a party, good music, and her favorite Liberian foods, such as potato greens, jollof rice, pepper soup, plantains, and a beautiful birthday cake. She said she could not remember a happier birthday.

Ngor Sarai has been part of my family all these years, encouraging me through full-time jobs, community college, and raising my boys. My brothers, sisters, and friends all know my sister, and her family knows about me. Through good times and hard times, she has been there, and I have always been there for her, too.

My family's most memorable vacation ever—a trip to Italy—was made possible by Ngor Sarai. At the time, she lived in the Consulate in Florence and invited us to stay with her for two amazing weeks, which we will never forget. We toured the area while Ngor Sarai worked, and on weekends she took us to places that filled our hearts with joy. On one such trip, we lost our way in the mountains. With the help of my oldest son, we read the map, and we found our way back to town. Every time we asked Ngor Sarai if we were lost, she would say, "No, we are on an adventure!" It is now a popular saying among my boys and me. If one of them says to me, "Mom, today I was on an adventure," or if I say it to them, we laugh, remember our sister and auntie, and explain how we found our way again.

Having such a loving sister in our lives sure tells how Peace Corps Liberia made an impact on my life, and I am forever grateful.

Elizabeth V. Sheriff grew up in Sierra Leone and returned to Liberia at twenty-four. She studied data entry, leading to work with CDC/USAID and the U.S. Embassy in Monrovia. During the heat of the war, Elizabeth entered the U.S. thanks to the "visa lottery," earned an associate degree, raised two boys, and has steadily worked multiple jobs—a proud U.S. citizen and proud West African.

BUMP IN THE NIGHT

BY REBEKAH SCHULZ

Liberia was dark. It was 2011 and I'll never forget my first night as a Peace Corps volunteer with my host family: I crawled into my mosquito tent, wrapped myself in my not-quite-big-enough fleece blanket, and switched off the dim, battery-powered lantern the Peace Corps had issued earlier that day. As my eyes adjusted to the darkness, I began to panic. My hand flew up to my face, feeling gingerly around my eyelids. I blinked a few times. Eyes open. Eyes closed. Eyes open. Eyes closed. There was no difference! I waved my hand in front of my face. Nothing. The darkness consumed all.

Many Peace Corps volunteers invested in generators to drive the darkness away, but within a few months I had come to appreciate it. In contrast to the frenetic days with no privacy and screaming children outside every window, the nights were a sanctuary. My roommate, Krista, and I started our wind-down routine around 7 p.m. with a candlelight dinner of whatever soupy concoction we'd cooked over the fire, followed by bucket baths. Night was largely considered a time to stay home, what with scorpions, snakes, and "heartmen" on the loose. I went back-and-forth on believing in the latter. A heartman worked for a medicine man, procuring the organs and body parts necessary for dark magic. Rumor had it that he accomplished this by abducting people walking alone at night. It seemed far-fetched, but every so often, the local radio station reported the discovery of a body with suspicious parts missing: a hole in the chest where a beating heart had been the day before, muscle and fascia where there should have been skin. It was enough to keep me inside at night, behind the barricaded front door and the metal window bars.

Our comfortable routine was shattered one evening about six weeks after we arrived in Sanniquellie. Krista retired early while I stayed up to grade math assignments. Finishing around 9 p.m., I slipped out of my clothes, wrapped a *lappa* around my chest, and walked to the bathroom with my bucket in one hand and a candle in the other. By Liberian standards, we had a nice indoor bathroom. The floor was bare concrete, but the walls were covered with small turquoise tiles to about eye-level, and the toilet even had a seat almost completely attached. Balanced on the pink water barrel, my candle illuminated the space romantically, and as I undressed, I could almost convince myself it was a rustic spa experience, the kind where you collected your own dust all day, then turned it into a full-body mud treatment.

Suddenly, just as my body was covered in soap, I heard something overhead. It flipped and flopped and scratched. I eyed the ceiling but continued to lather, trying to ignore the aggressive thuds advancing in my direction. "La la la . . ." I whispered to distract myself, nevertheless eyeing a slim crack above my head where the ceiling didn't quite meet the wall. *My hand could barely fit through there*, I thought. "La la la . . ."

Just then something burst through the crack! All I saw was motion and all I heard was my screams. *Was this how it happened? Could a heartman shapeshift and attack people in their homes?* At this point, anything seemed possible, and I braced for the end. It bounced off my left shoulder and took flight, chaotically circling the tiny room with its two-foot wingspan. I fled and the door slammed behind me. There I was: naked, covered in soap in the dark. Eyes open. Eyes closed. Nothing. I knew Krista must have heard my screams, but her room was silent. I felt my way down the hall to her door. "Krista," I hissed. Nothing. "Krista!" I ducked behind the wall to hide my nakedness as she opened the door a crack. "What's going on?" she whispered. "I heard you screaming."

I begged her for a *lappa*, and once I was covered, I tried to explain. "Something fell out of the ceiling! It flies and its wings are nearly two feet!" I decided not to mention that it could be a heartman in disguise. She squinted her eyes in disbelief, but just then the flailing and thrashing started up again. "Fine," she said resolutely, "I'll go look."

Brandishing a broom, she eased the bathroom door open a crack. "I see your glasses on the floor." She opened it a little wider and stepped inside. I peered in behind her and saw what was making all the noise: a large bat was collapsed on its back next to the toilet. It thrashed menacingly and we retreated in a fit of nervous laughter.

After a combined pep talk and strategy session, we decided the only option was to trap it. Krista rushed in and slammed an empty bucket over it, and we piled algebra textbooks on top to secure it. Flip, flop, scratch. It held! I quickly rinsed the soap off my body, keeping one eye fixed on the bucket and then crawled into bed with my adrenaline still pumping.

We left the bat under the bucket for two full days until, after Krista had relayed the story a dozen times, one of the other volunteers accused us of animal cruelty.

"It's probably rabid," I argued. "We are doing a public service."

Nonetheless, later that week Krista opened the back door and shoved the bucket toward it. I wasn't home at the time so I can't say with certainty, but Krista claims that as she swatted the bat out the door it grabbed hold of the stick and took flight. Horrified at the thought of its survival, I combed the backyard but found no bat bodies.

I've often wondered about that bat. Was it rabid or just confused? In the end, it wasn't the darkness that surprised me as much as what emerged from it. What looks like nothing is rarely nothing, especially when it goes bump in the night.

Rebekah Schulz was a Peace Corps volunteer in Liberia from 2011 to 2013. She taught math at Sanniquellie Central High. She later moved to Suakoko and worked on a USAID project at Cuttington University. After returning to the United States, she earned a master's degree in international education from Harvard University and currently works as a consultant in Washington, D.C.

A MOTHER'S LOVE

BY NIMU SIDHU

Vaye Town Public School sits atop a large hill deep in the Liberian bush. Each morning, a tall pole awaits the glory of the Liberian flag for the morning devotion—the pledge of allegiance, prayers, and songs.

In 2013, my day as a Peace Corps math and science teacher was three hours long, nonstop. It is perhaps no surprise that my first period eighth-grade students were my favorite. They had an adolescent, boisterous sass that never crossed the line of disrespect. Florence feigned disciplining younger students, Jebelu constantly volunteered, and Benjamin emulated Jebelu. Mabel and Kumba formed my girls' math squad. But the mix of students changed daily—health and economic hardship had half the students out on a typical day.

A month after school started, Mustapha showed up for the first time. At fifteen years old, he was a tad scrawny, but with his carefully pressed uniform and wide, observant eyes, he appeared to be a sincere student. When I taught the shortcut conversion of percentages to decimals, most students were satisfied after two examples. Skeptical Mustapha continued to perform the conversion using long division until he was fully convinced.

It was another two weeks before I saw Mustapha again. Due to his absences, he barely passed my class. He remembered everything from the days that he did attend, and on tests he would write, "I don't know this, but I would please like to learn." I learned that Mustapha was an orphan living with his auntie, a cook shop owner, who mistreated and overworked him.

Two months later, another Peace Corps volunteer asked me to help plan and run a national science fair. It involved a mentor-mentee team per school and a scientific method-based investigation into a topic of the student's choice. I was nervous to ask Mustapha about it. I barely knew him, and how could I justify selecting him over the other students? When I finally mustered the courage, he replied, "I don't have time . . . I don't earn high marks in science . . . find someone better."

I was heartbroken and reluctant to ask other wonderful students to participate. As I was coming to terms with his rejection, Mustapha came back to me. He had reconsidered and wanted to learn everything that I wanted to teach. "Even if I don't understand, there must be some reason you have asked me."

Our journey started with us reading about different science topics in the evening hours on my porch. We found comfort in simply reading aloud. It was a rare time for us to quiet our background worries.

After making our way through a 1990s children's science text, Mustapha declared his interest in motor neurons. Like all of my students, he had never conducted a single experiment, but came to design his own in which my only role was utilizing the Socratic Method. Mustapha's experiment had two components: to investigate how age affects hand-eye coordination using a watch, needle, and thread, and to investigate how age affects memory using a unique set of words and a simple point system for short- and long-term recollection.

For the next month, we collected data from the community. He came up with explanations for our results, such as the real effects of sleep and stress on memory as uncontrolled variables. He even arrived at the concept of an outlier on his own.

To attend the science fair, we traveled for one day through the capital city and beyond. Mustapha was completely out of his village element. He had never touched a computer, so I helped him complete his PowerPoint presentation. No surprise to anyone present, Mustapha won the Science Fair championship. One judge called him "Liberia's first and foremost neuroscientist."

Mustapha, whom I began to refer to as "my son," started to ask me complex questions about human nature and the world. We'd discuss how children could best deal with difficult situations, specifically those imposed by the adults who are supposed to care for them. By then, I was familiar with his auntie's reputation. He had dropped out of school right before the fair because she refused to pay his school fees, but I had him readmitted. At that time, he said, "You're not just the best teacher I've had, but my best friend."

Then Mustapha went missing. He never sat for any of his tests and stopped coming by to read. Almost two weeks later, Mustapha came to me and explained, "My auntie plans to leave her husband and wants to build a new house. She is having wood chopped deep in the bush and is forcing me and other children to carry the loads to the building site. I told her I was tired, and then she starved me for three days. I waited under the mango trees for ripe ones to drop—too tired to climb."

There wasn't much I could say. I tried to comfort him and talked about the injustice and why it was so important for him to have opportunities. I lightly scolded him for not coming to me for food. But then I did exactly what I would have otherwise despised. I had him readmitted to school, this time asking all the teachers to falsify his grades so he could pass into ninth grade. Even so, I still shamed the teachers for giving Mustapha portions of labor rather than edifying make-up assignments. Finally, I paid the common bribery fee to "free" Mustapha's passing report card, allowing him to register for the ninth grade.

That summer, an Ebola outbreak forced volunteers to evacuate Liberia. Mustapha and I had a very uncertain and challenging goodbye. Over a year later, when schools reopened, his auntie would not allow him to return. A fire stirred in me. From an ocean away, with the help of another volunteer and the principal of another school, I maneuvered to free Mustapha from his living situation.

Mustapha now lives in the Liberian capital and will graduate high school. Everything that my mom said about "a mother's love" is true. He will always be my son.

Nimu Sidhu was in the fourth group of Peace Corps volunteers to return to Liberia after the civil wars. She was a math and chemistry teacher at a public school in Vaye Town, Gbarpolu County, from 2013 to 2014. She has a degree in biophysics and works as a data scientist in Washington, D.C. Nimu enjoys cooking, hiking, and dancing.

ORDINARY PEOPLE DO EXTRAORDINARY THINGS

BY SALLY GOSLINE HUMPHREY

It was 1963. My Peace Corps partner and I were settling into Liberian village life. We lived in a small Muslim village called Tumutu, about fifty miles from the capital of Monrovia, on the main road upcountry, and taught in a government primary school a mile away. It wasn't long before we met Amah and his younger brother, Mori. In those days, many people in Liberia didn't know exactly how old they were. Amah was probably about thirty and Mori was about thirteen. They took us under their wings and helped us settle into their village.

Amah taught me how to carry a live chicken under my arm, like the one that was gifted to us when we visited his uncle. He also showed me how to butcher and de-feather it. With the help of others, he built a "palaver hut" next to our house where we taught reading and writing to the children from Tumutu. In the evenings, once the sun had set, a group of young boys and girls came for their lessons.

Like all young boys, Mori helped his family clear the bush to plant rice and cassava every year. As the plants ripened, the boys frightened the birds away with their slingshots. Mori didn't go to the government school. Instead, he went to the Islamic school in the village.

One day, Mori asked how he might be able to make some money. We thought about it together. The children who went to the government school walked through Tumutu every day on their way to and from the school. "I wonder if you could make something the children might like to buy?"

A few days later, Mori ran into our house. "I have an idea. I could make a bread oven and bake sweet bread rolls to sell to the children as they walk past."

Soon a mound of mud, like a pizza oven, grew in a space between two houses. With the new oven, Mori started to make and sell sweet bread rolls for a penny each. The school children loved them. He eventually made a hundred and ninety dollars and used it to plant a few orange and rubber trees at the edge of the village.

I completed my Peace Corps service in June of 1965. Forty-seven years later, in 2012, I had the chance to visit Liberia again. After almost five decades and two civil wars, I wondered if my village was still there. I searched for Amah and Mori in Tumutu. In 1996, Charles Taylor's troops had marched down the main road, which runs right through the village. Those were terrible years for everyone.

I asked my taxi driver to go slowly as we drove into Tumutu. It was difficult to remember; it was so long ago. Suddenly, I spotted my house. It was still there! It didn't look very well cared for, but it was there. I quickly climbed up the bank and walked around it. In a flash, there was a crowd of older women and lots of small children surrounding me. "I lived here nearly fifty years ago and taught in the school," I explained. "I was Peace Corps."

The older women burst out laughing. They actually remembered me, and soon, I recognized them. I asked them about Amah and Mori. "Yes. Follow me," they answered. My heart jumped. Were they still alive?

We walked past several thatched houses, and there, sitting on a worn-out hammock, just like the one he had woven for me years ago, was Amah. He looked old. His clothes were ragged. And he was blind. Even though he couldn't see, Amah was very busy skillfully weaving thin wires together to make fish traps.

"What happened?" I immediately asked.

One of the boys explained, "Years ago, before the civil war, Amah worked on a rubber farm. There was a fight, and he was blinded. He has two wives who take good care of him and everyone in the village looks after him too."

I sat down next to Amah on the hammock, but he was completely confused. After forty-two years living in England, I had lost my American accent. He didn't believe it was me. Finally, people convinced him it really was me, and he wept. He couldn't believe I had come back, and I couldn't believe he was still alive. The young boy continued, "When Charles Taylor's fighters came through the village, everyone ran into the bush, but Amah couldn't run. He hid in his house. It was amazing he wasn't killed."

Amah spoke up. "I stayed five days and five nights without food or water until finally people came back from the bush."

Tears of joy slowly slid down my cheeks.

Sally returned to Tumutu in 2012 and found her friends

While we were talking, a few small boys had been sent to find Mori, who was working in his field. When we saw each other, we couldn't stop smiling. Young Mori had grown into a fine man. He proudly introduced me to his teenage son and daughter and explained that his wife was out selling oranges in the market. He took me to see the house he had built—a fine house with an impressive carved wooden door. He also showed me the latrine he was building out of mud bricks, and the orange and rubber trees he had planted so long ago.

I spotted a small structure made of sticks with soil on top. "What's that?"

"That's where I grew rubber trees from seeds. My son and I cleared a large field and planted twenty-five hundred rubber trees. It will take five years before I can take any latex. I plan to sell the latex to a cooperative rubber factory not far away. The trees should eventually make a ton of latex a month, which could earn my family fifteen hundred dollars a month."

I wasn't surprised to find that Mori had hatched this grand scheme, or that Amah was making fish traps, even though he was blind. They had both lived through times without enough food to eat, times without enough water to bathe, and a long civil war that was "horrible" in the words of their sister. In spite of all the difficult times they had been through, these two ordinary people managed to do extraordinary things.

Sally Gosline Humphrey taught at Martha Tubman Elementary School in Salala as a Peace Corps volunteer from 1963 to 1965. She returned to the U.S. to teach elementary school in Berkeley, California. In 1970, she moved with her husband to Oxford, England, where she taught English to ethnic minorities and refugees. She enjoys biking, Balkan dancing, gardening, and especially spending time with her two grandchildren.

THE CONCERNED WOMEN OF WEAMAWUO

BY NIMU SIDHU

Weamawuo, which means "on the river," is a two hundred-person village along a long dirt road that climbs through the bush all the way up to Sierra Leone. Weamawuo is between four and eight hours from the coastal capital—depending whether it's rainy season or dry season.

In the rainy season, rain thrashes upon zinc roofs. Liberians tease, "De rain will flog you!" The rain opens up muddy potholes along the curvy road. Sometimes the murky water reaches a depth of two feet, covering dozens of yards. But in the dry season, clothes bake in the sun, and a tan dust settles on everything. Dry season brings an economic revival: colossal trees are chopped and hauled, miners flock to the quarries and riverbeds, and small goods like homemade beverages, snacks, and meat begin to sell at higher prices.

Dry season activities add very heavy vehicles to the already increased traffic through Weamawuo. Mothers, alarmed, scold playing kids to get out of the road. Safety is most precarious along the Weamawuo Bridge. The longest bridge in Liberia, its single lane spans a quarter-mile. Made of weathered and worn wooden planks, the bridge hangs precariously sixty feet above the Lofa River, which dwindles to reveal the exposed rocky riverbed in dry season and gushes rapids in rainy season.

I was terrified the first time I walked across the bridge. In 2013, during my first dry season, the extra traffic—trucks carrying mining equipment and massive logs—damaged the rotten wood so that it teetered on the brink of collapse. Entire planks were missing. Sometimes stepping on one end of a plank would raise it from the other end.

Soon, residents living on either side of the bridge refused to cross on foot. The clever, small boys of the village parsed a safe foot path across and capitalized on this for a small fee. Truck drivers, however, had no choice but to learn to maneuver across in order to supply essential food and small goods. Weamawuo Bridge was the only way across for hours and miles in any direction.

With school on one side of the river, many students crossed the bridge on foot every morning. Two years earlier, a small girl had fallen through the bridge on her way to school. She was lucky to fall into the bush and had survived. But now, with the bridge crumbling, the community was simmering: "The bridge done spoil-o. It looking to come and jus' fall down." The Concerned Women of Weamawuo—two self-organized women's groups, one on either side of the bridge—made an executive decision: "We closin' de bridge. Only de feet can pass. De government will have no choice, dey must come, or what shame dey will face."

This was not any ordinary protest. The women needed to guard the bridge from both sides at all hours, day and night. On the eve of the protest at a storefront gathering, a fellow teacher jokingly beckoned, "Sis Hawa, you will join de women to sleep on de bridge?"

I had originally intended to show my support after school only. But I said simply, "All the women will be there."

Everyone at the storefront froze. One woman, Jumah, burst out, "You?!"

But then, everyone was smiling, and another woman, Hasunatu, roared with pride, "What, you think Sis Hawa is not Weamawuo woman? How she different from us? She know we will lead her."

I went home to prepare: had my bucket bath, doused myself in mosquito repellant, and readied myself for the cold, dry-season night—desert-like, with the wind ripping by the river. The women had laid out large pieces of cardboard and woven bamboo mats. A smoky fire burned on one end, and people sold small foodstuffs like meat soup—bush-meat in a tear-jerking, spicy broth—out of buckets. Word had spread. Everyone was alive, and the night was young.

Those first evenings were filled with dancing—heels rhythmically beating into the wooden bridge—and harmonic tribal chants. It was invigorating to be around these women. But it was not easy or simple. This was a protest, after all. At first, drivers tried to bribe us. They became irritated as the days of protest turned into weeks, causing indefinite reroutes. Some threatened to drive over us, and one man defecated near us on the bridge. The women, however, were so unified that each one supported the others, like a spiritual scaffold.

After my first night on the bridge, my students eagerly gossiped and approached me to confirm: "You, Sis Hawa? You sleep there?" Some of my students started to visit me on the bridge, and we would talk into the night. It was fascinating for them to see me in that setting, late at night with the other women, sleeping side-by-side.

Within one week, the national radio station was pulsating with news of the bridge closing—miners are powerful people. The Concerned Women leader came up to me proudly, "We told you dey will hear us!" The whole village was talking about what we were going to accomplish, together, for the families and for the children who depended on this bridge.

After two more weeks of protests, UN peacekeepers arrived. Negotiations with the Concerned Women leaders began. Naturally, cheaper wooden planks were initially proposed. But after another week, the pounding and hammering of fresh wooden planks onto the bridge frame resonated throughout Weamawuo.

The Concerned Women had won!

Nimu Sidhu was in the fourth group of Peace Corps volunteers to return to Liberia after the civil wars. She was a math and chemistry teacher at a public school in Vaye Town, Gbarpolu County, from 2013 to 2014. She has a degree in biophysics and works as a data scientist in Washington, D.C. Nimu enjoys cooking, hiking, and dancing.

PEACE CORPS GOALS AND LIBERIAN WAYS

BY MAXWELL SINES

The Peace Corps has three goals, loosely paraphrased: send well-trained volunteers to a willing country, blend cultures, and be the voice for other cultures in the United States. Liberians could condense these into three phrases: "Take time," "Let's eat," and "How'd you sleep?"

TAKE TIME

A Liberian saying is sometimes uttered after the fact, yet it reflects the pace of the country. Liberians move to their individual clocks and won't be rushed. As a Silicon Valley kid, the slower vibe and consistent inconsistency of my post, Tappita, was frustrating until I took the time to understand my journey in Liberia.

There is no such thing as "late" in Liberia. All cell phones are reset daily at a charging station for ten Liberian dollars (about fifteen U.S. cents), and a casual encounter on the road can last from five minutes to five hours. Schools were delayed days or weeks. My first five months in-country, I struggled daily with impatience. I would rush to school just to wait. It was during one of these waits that Liberian "time" truly sunk in.

I was running late and anxious because I had stressed punctuality to my students. As my fear built, my anger intensified at the market lady who had waylaid me by discussing why her country rice was the best. As I was running, I made the crucial mistake of taking my eyes off the path and ended up in a ditch.

"Take time," said a Liberian Samaritan as he helped me out of the mud. He told me that all a person has to give in their life is their time. He reminded me that I had taken years in preparation to reach Liberia. He reiterated that Liberians move at their own speed and are never crunched for time. He taught me that a life can be extended if we appreciate our moments.

Thank you for helping me understand "taking time."

LET'S EAT

"Let's eat" are words of love in Liberia and also in the U.S. for my grandmother. The phrase embodies Liberian generosity and provided a way for me to assimilate. I believed then, and do now, that food and the traditions that surround it are as vital to the souls of societies as to their stomachs.

I grew up with monthly gatherings where all the generations of my entire family would mash around a table for four. Converted ironing boards became the kids' table. We made it work, we squeezed, we shrank, we ate in the garage, on the washer, on the floor. We had enough food to share. Food made with love became the centerpiece of wonderful family memories.

I witnessed the decline of food traditions in my own culture. The availability of frozen meals and franchise dining dramatically increased. Fast-food became a lifestyle, power was converted into snack bars, and essential nutrients were blended and liquefied to save time. Meals, no longer shared, were consumed rapidly, leading to a decline in traditional family gatherings. Tappita allowed me to refocus on the importance of food, not just *what* goes into my body, but *how* as well.

Liberians generously offered their food with conversation in between heaping spoonfuls of rice. I reconnected to my own history and shared my Sicilian heritage, expanding on the second goal of the Peace Corps. I shared mounds of pasta, hospitality, conversation, and country wine. I returned to a time when food gratified not only my stomach but my soul as well.

When cooking, I was frustrated to have to wait for the coals to heat up as the fire "caught." However, that little bit of waiting gave way to unscripted conversations. We listened to each other and became a community. My Sicilian grandmother was pleased to learn that during my service, I never ate alone, and that her famous mish-mash, Depression-era recipe was sustaining for Tappita neighbors and travelers alike.

"Let's eat. Let us build a community."

"Let's eat" was my welcome home.

HOW'D YOU SLEEP?

Such a personal question to ask in the United States. Sleep in my native country is viewed as a tedious necessity to break up the workdays, not as a true blessing of faith and trust.

The greeting of "How'd you sleep?" is used in Liberia as a daily confirmation, asked not in search of the amount of time or the dreams, or even the activity of the huge rats who used the dark at their discretion. It was a reminder that we survived the night, when we were most vulnerable. The question in itself is a testimony to our existence, and allows for the opportunity to enjoy this life together. My initial reaction to this question was: "Where do I start?"

The unbearable heat? A running tummy due to spoiled bush meat? The buzzing mosquitoes possibly carrying malaria? The freaky anti-malarial mefloquine-fueled dreams? The thin, folded foam mattress between my sweaty body and the cold concrete floor? The intrusion of frolicking cockroaches? I powered through my night with the help of the local gin and Benadryl pills—my sleep aides those first few months. How'd I sleep? I slept like shit!

My upbringing taught me enough manners not to divulge my soul at every question, and as my first days in Tappita became weeks, turning into months and years, "How'd you sleep?" replaced my daily "Wass-up?" I started to understand the phrase as a reference to surviving the vulnerability of sleep.

I'd arrived in a Liberia recovering from decades of civil war. For the Liberians who survived that war, "How'd you sleep?" showed their immense appreciation for each moment. It was a reminder that they made it to *this* moment, together. That *death*, disguised as dysentery, malaria, or warlords did not make their rest permanent. My Liberian friends shared with me the ability to appreciate the blessing of community and knowledge that our *past* continuously shapes us, yet those nightmarish moments will never deny us our *future* gifts of joy.

"How'd you sleep?"
"How'd you live?"

Maxwell Sines arrived in Liberia as one of the first Peace Corps volunteers to return to the country after the civil wars. He taught physics in Tappita, Nimba County, from 2010 to 2012. Maxwell received his teaching credential upon returning to his native San José and has been teaching physics, math, and Liberian history to all available ears across the Silicon Valley.

KU MENI JU, MY FRIEND?

BY PAUL EAGLE

1988

Dave Kontoe is riding on the back of my motorcycle as we navigate the muddy roads of the rainy season. He's my unofficial Peace Corps counterpart, helping translate my imperfect Liberian English with farmers, teaching me Kpelle, the local language, and explaining how to work and live in this Liberian town. On this day, we are checking on our fish farmers in the region. He easily slips in and out of several languages while talking to the farmers. He effortlessly wields a cutlass to chop up a mango, then hands out chunks to the gaggle of children following us around. He packs the mud of a fishpond bank with a palm frond and catches chickens in his weathered hands to check their vitals. We stop to buy red palm oil at Joseph Mulbah's shop, then continue the ride to Dave's farm to check out his pigs and fish.

Mami Lorpu calls us for dinner, and we eat her famous palm butter soup. Served over rice, it is the freshest sauce and chicken I will ever eat. The rains have brought cool air and we sit soaking it in as day turns into evening. Suffering continues in Belefanai, and all across Liberia. But for the first time in a decade, after a 1980 military coup and a 1985 rigged election and attempted coup, seemingly, there is peace and stability in the country. People are optimistic about the new "kol tar" or paved road that will connect Gbarnga and Voinjama. More area farmers have begun fish farming, and a record number of children now attend the town's schools in their pressed blue-and-yellow uniforms. Peace Corps has nearly two hundred volunteers in the country.

1989

The first sign I see of danger is at the Tuesday market in Gbarnga—just a month after a small rebel incursion in December that is growing quickly. Bright yellow-and-purple *lappa* cloth decorates market stalls; tables are spread with piles of peanuts, rice, and peppers; and women carry large pans of bush meat (forest antelope, monkey, and snake). Suddenly, three loud cracks, clearly gunfire, bring the buzz and bustle of the market to an abrupt halt. We all freeze and look at each other. In the next moment, the women are wrapping all their food into *lappas* and running in all directions. Screams, crying, and chaos ensue, and within minutes, the market is completely empty. A Lebanese merchant tells me later that a government soldier fired his gun in the air, and no one was injured. But it is the first of many signs that I will be going home soon. Over the next several months, rebels invade eastern Liberia and begin fighting their way toward the capital city of Monrovia. It's the beginning of two devastating civil wars that will last fifteen years.

2018

The tires of the Toyota Land Cruiser slip and spin in the red mud; nothing is slicker than roads in the rainy season in Liberia. Woodsmoke hangs in the humid air and chickens sprint along the roadside as we follow an enormous Mandingo-owned truck filled with white bags of rice and charcoal, red-and-blue pig-foot barrels strapped to its sides, and an old motorcycle lashed with rubber ties to its back end. We pass an imposing billboard warning us about the recent Ebola virus that killed nearly five thousand Liberians. Mile after mile, mud and stick homes stand stripped of their zinc-metal roofs, reminders of the war that finally ended five years before.

It's been thirty years since I last saw Dave Kontoe. Over the years, we exchanged a couple of letters and spoke once or twice on the phone. I still feel guilty about the way we Peace Corps volunteers left the country, abandoning our friends as the war erupted around us, and about my spotty communication over the decades. Now I'm in Liberia for work and have managed to fit in a trip back to Belefanai. The Land Cruiser finally arrives at the town and stops on the Gbarnga-Voinjama highway. Dave approaches me as we stop in front of his family farm. Amazingly, I was able to reach one of his relatives on Facebook who alerted him that I would be visiting this Saturday morning, and he is waiting. I recognize his smile instantly. He seems fragile, with several teeth missing and an old beige sweatshirt hanging from his frail frame. He limps toward me in his flip-flops, gives me a Liberian finger-snap handshake and hug, and says, "*Ku meni ju*, my friend?" He's asking me "what news?" in Kpelle, and we both laugh at the absurdity of trying to catch up after three decades. I feel a big lump in my throat.

He takes me first to see the graves—carved, white concrete stones in the thick green bush: Mami Lorpu, the leader of her family and the market women; Old Man Mathew, my kind friend and landlord. They both died in exile in the U.S. More tombstones, more familiar names. Dave takes me to his house, a small, mud-walled shack with a leaking zinc roof, where I meet his wife, kids, and grandkids, and am given the traditional Liberian welcome with a kola nut, a chicken, and a twenty-five cent coin. Then, in the pouring rain, Dave takes me for a tour of his piggery and fishponds. Once thriving businesses, the fishponds are now dried up and overgrown and the piggery has been stripped of every usable piece of lumber and metal roofing. Dave has tried to rebuild a semblance of his piggery with the materials at hand—mud, wires, sticks, and palm branches. He tells me that when the rebels invaded his village, he took his family and hid in the bush for months, eating leaves, bamboo worms, and whatever else they could scrounge. He lost a child and witnessed numerous relatives being executed. Like many Liberians, he is still haunted by these memories.

I return to the States a few weeks later. With the help of former Peace Corps volunteers who served in Belefanai, and a few family members, we will raise enough money for Dave to rebuild his piggery and we will continue to stay in touch. But on this day, thirty years later, over potato greens, rice, and Coca-Cola, we laugh about crashing our motorcycle off a bridge, fishponds that wouldn't drain, and palm wine that gave us "running belly." I marvel at Dave's resilience and his gratitude after so much suffering. And together, we feel joy.

Paul Eagle was a Peace Corps volunteer from 1988 to 1990 in Belefanai, Bong County, where he worked at a radio station and built fishponds. He currently serves as vice-president of marketing and communications at Catholic Relief Services, one of the largest humanitarian agencies in the world. Paul is an avid runner and record collector.

FORTY-ONE

BY ELOISE ANNETTE CAMPBELL

Heaven and Earth came together in a little town called Fortsville, Liberia. I didn't see it at first. But then I came to appreciate it some years later.

From the beginning, I resisted Liberia's charm. My fear and lack of knowledge blurred my vision. After all, I arrived in Monrovia in 1973 with not much more than a blow dryer and electric curlers in hand, for heaven's sake. I arrived as part of Teaching Group 41, which would become my lucky number through life as well as during the birth of my three sons.

I met a fellow volunteer who changed my outlook. He was opposite in personality from me, embracing all things positive in Liberia. I was sent to Owensgrove in Bassa County, and my friend, to Fortsville. Lucky for me, the towns were only twenty minutes apart.

During my first trip to Fortsville, my friend introduced me to the Reverend and Mrs. Gardner, an older missionary couple teaching both civil education and the word of God. Their large, corrugated tin home was perched on the main road, connecting Harbel to Buchanan. I recall the Gardners having an organ in the center of the house. Their joyful music filled the rooms with love and comfort. Mrs. Gardner happily playing the organ always reminded me of Doc in the fairy tale of Snow White, filling the dwarfs' cottage with joy and laughter. The Gardners embodied all that was good. They were generous, kind, funny, and smart, and helped raise some of the local children.

But the most blessed jewel of Fortsville lived just down the road. Her name was Odelia Gant. She was eighty or so but looked ninety. She was a tiny, frail lady with light-colored eyes. In spite of a long tooth prominent in the top front of her mouth, because there were no bottom teeth to abut it, she was strikingly beautiful. I regret not having quality photos of her instead of the grainy, unfocused pics I took at the time. I often begged her to pose for a photograph, but she refused. Finally, one day she consented, and after spending some time dressing in a button-up dress, she posed, stone-faced.

Life was hard for most people in Fortsville, and even more so for Odelia. She was tough as nails and raising a small Liberian girl not much older than four. OD, as she preferred to be called, lived in a house on stilts, a common style in Bassa County. OD was constantly up and down the stairs. When we visited, we usually sat outside near the outdoor kitchen of corrugated tin. OD chopped her own wood, carried it bundled on her head and cooked a mean fufu with smoked fish stew. I must say that I have not had finer home-cooked food since.

She had scrawny laying chickens for eggs. Every morning when she gathered eggs, she claimed mites from the nests crawled into her ears and tickled them, keeping her up at night. So, every now and then, she would spray Shelltox directly in her ears. Shelltox was a strong insecticide found in local stores. I suggested she shouldn't do that, but she laughed and shrugged off my advice. After all, she was over eighty and going strong.

A rocking chair sat on her front porch. She claimed her great-grandmother had been a former slave in the U.S. who had immigrated to Liberia. The great-grandmother had been quite elderly, so the family dragged her around on this rocking chair until the runners were worn flat.

I left Bassa County for Ganta for my second year of teaching. OD was devastated and we wept hard that day. But I returned several times to visit and stayed in her home. I recall not sleeping very well with cockroaches buzzing around and plopping on my bed. I was awake for most of the night. OD made a good cup of coffee, since half of the cup was sweetened condensed milk. She couldn't get enough of the stuff. I made sure I brought several cans every time I visited.

When it was time for me to leave Liberia, I stopped to visit OD one last time. I didn't tell her that I was leaving Liberia, as I thought she would be heartbroken. But the tears running down my cheeks told OD that something was about to change. I loved her more than I can describe. I thank God every day for what she taught me: to let go of unimportant things and embrace the gift of love and friendship.

Later in life, I was blessed with three incredible sons. They were born at 8:41 a.m., 1:41 p.m., and 2:41 a.m. I was born at 2:41 p.m. Forty-one has become our lucky number and was certainly mine. Group 41 changed my life for the better. I came to settle in another Heaven on Earth at the forty-first latitudinal line.

In 2009, I returned to Liberia. I hired a taxi and stopped by Fortsville. I didn't recognize the place. I desperately tried to find a familiar sight but never found one. The church that I didn't recall being there was riddled with bullet holes from the civil war and most of the houses were gone. When I asked about OD, a small child took me to a residence and told me to wait. A woman emerged and informed me that the angels had come to take Odelia Gant to heaven in the late 1980s. This woman happened to be OD's niece. I gave her the hand-crocheted shawl I had brought for OD. She caressed it with a tear in her eye, so like OD's face thirty-three years before.

After Eloise Annette Campbell taught math and sciences in Ganta and Owensgrove, Liberia, in Group 41, from 1973 to 1975, she traveled extensively through West Africa, Kenya, Tanzania, and Egypt. She returned to Ohio, received her Juris Doctorate degree, represented indigents through Legal Aid, and was a court-appointed special advocate for neglected children. Eloise enjoys sailing and boating on Lake Erie with her family.

RIPPING OUT THE SEAMS

BY REBEKAH SCHULZ

Oretha, the bartender at the Cuttington University canteen, knew everything and everyone. We quickly became close friends, and one sunny day in 2014, during the height of dry season, I invited her to my house. Over my weak version of pepper soup, my heart spoke, "Do you know any good tailors? I want to learn to sew."

Sewing had been my dream since, as a Peace Corps volunteer trainee three years earlier, I first visited a Liberian tailor and learned they sewed without patterns. The next morning, Oretha returned with Mistress Yekeh, and my life was forever changed.

The same age as my mother, Mistress Yekeh was slim and barely five feet tall, but immediately filled a room with her warm personality and impeccable African suits. She made them all herself, having taught tailoring at a vocational school before the Liberian civil war. Trying to make a new start fourteen years later, Mistress Yekeh got a job at the university library and was working toward a degree in education. She no longer sewed professionally but was willing to help me so she could finish plastering her house. I paid her ten U.S. dollars every Sunday, and each time she smiled and said, "Another bag of cement!"

I bought my own sewing machine, and Mistress Yekeh came over on the weekends to teach me her secrets. We laid out bed sheets or old curtains on the living room floor, sketched a design in yellow chalk, then inevitably cut holes in my floor mat. Each week, she left me with an assignment, and seven days later, I presented it for inspection. Without fail, Mistress Yekeh would drop her head and try unsuccessfully to hold back a babbling stream of laughter.

Eventually, she'd compose herself and say, "It's good for a learner. You tried. You *actually* tried." Then she'd throw it back in my lap. "Now, tear out the seams. That's the only way you will learn to do it right."

Some weeks I'd protest, "But it's on the inside! I'm the only one who will know!"

She always had the same response, "If you let yourself do bad work, that's all you'll ever do. Try to be perfect. Then you'll feel proud."

Reluctantly, I followed orders.

Rip.

As school restarted and the semester got busy, we had fewer lessons, but I still saw her almost every day. She left the library to walk to her village around the same time I struggled to haul my bags up the hill in my tight *lappa* skirt.

"Heeeeey, African woman!" she'd yell, "Did you finish your assignment yet?"

I would shake my head and laugh, she would shake her head and laugh, and we'd both continue home.

It was 2014, and Ebola was spreading through Guinea, but everything remained business as usual, both in Liberia and on the USAID project where I worked.

"I won't worry until the Peace Corps volunteers leave," I told my worried colleagues.

Things felt so normal, I even planned a vacation home. I haphazardly threw some T-shirts in a bag, and, six months after my sewing lessons began, left without saying a single goodbye. Two days after I landed in the U.S., the Peace Corps evacuated volunteers, the university closed, and my project paused. Suddenly, I found myself displaced to Missouri. Mistress Yekeh traveled to Monrovia to be with her daughter and elderly mother.

A few weeks later, all three of them died of Ebola: First, the daughter, then the mother, then finally, Mistress Yekeh. A colleague from the library told me she lay on the ground outside an overcrowded treatment center. She never made it inside and rests instead in an unmarked mass grave on the outskirts of the capital.

The day I heard the news, I sat in my parents' basement, mindlessly scrolling through Facebook, searching in vain for a cat video to distract me from my grief. Something caught my eye. "Now it's getting serious! [laugh emoji]" a friend said, tagging an NPR article titled, "Should You Stock Up on Chocolate Bars Because of Ebola?" I foolishly clicked, like someone rubber-necking an interstate pileup, and learned the price of an average Hershey's bar had increased by five to ten cents.

Thousands are dead from Ebola, and *now* it's getting serious?

Rip. Rip. RIP.

At fifty-seven, Mistress Yekeh had seen the worst side of humanity and the hardest side of life during Liberia's civil wars . . . and survived to laugh about it. But the difference between violence and viruses is that everyone knows how to run from bullets: grab your family and go. Ebola, however, came quietly and killed painfully. Without enough treatment centers, families were asked to literally watch their loved ones die before their eyes. I am certain that when Mistress Yekeh's mother and daughter fell ill the *last* thing she was thinking was to run. In Liberia, family is everything and the tragedy of Ebola was that the tighter that bond, the more people loved and cared for each other, the more deadly the disease became.

I eventually returned to Liberia and stayed nearly three more years. But my sewing machine collected dust, my last assignment, half-stitched where we'd left it, the needle frozen midair as if waiting for Mistress Yekeh's return. My foot often caught in the many holes we'd made in the floor mat.

Rip.

Today, I work four thousand miles away as an international development consultant. At the start of the COVID-19 pandemic, my team was asked to research responses for schools and their eyes turned to me.

"We need to know about Ebola," a colleague said flatly.

My breath caught in my chest as I heard Mistress Yekeh's laughter and saw her strong, veined hands tugging at my cloth. Here we go again.

Rip.

How many people lined up at hospitals in 2020, unsure if they could get COVID treatment? How many people were told to isolate from their own families? Is the world simply unraveling, or is some higher power tugging at our seams?

"If you let yourself do bad work, that's all you'll ever do."

Let that be our call to action.

Let's stitch back a world we can be proud of.

Rebekah Schulz was a Peace Corps volunteer in Liberia from 2011 to 2013. She taught math at Sanniquellie Central High. She later moved to Suakoko and worked on a USAID project at Cuttington University. After returning to the United States, she earned a master's degree in international education from Harvard University and currently works as a consultant in Washington, D.C.

GOD SAVED THE WHITE WOMAN

BY VICTORIA ZAWITKOWSKI

I had never been called "white" before, except in boxes that I checked on a standardized test. That was the only way people in Liberia described me, unless they mistook me for a Chinese woman—or sometimes a Chinese man. It felt like an accusation. Early in my Peace Corps volunteer assignment, I hated everyone staring at me as I walked down the street or shopped at the market. I hated when people stopped outside my classroom, giggling about "the white woman teaching." I shooed them away, claiming they were disturbing the class, but really, they were disturbing me.

I had been in Liberia for almost two years on that fateful day in 2019. In fact, I was going to the goodbye ceremony my school had planned for me in my home village of Sanoyea. That day, I had been working at the training center in Kakata, a major trading city that lies on the path of the country's only highway. My hour-and-a-half journey home was split equally between a taxi and a motorbike ride. I was one of the lucky ones, as many volunteers traveled distances far greater and dustier than mine. I rushed to get back to my village to put on my fine *lappa* and be on time for the ceremony in my honor.

I made my way to the chaotic Kakata taxi station, where vehicles were everywhere with drivers looking for passengers. The goal was to find the one with the most paying customers, so they could be the first to leave. Drivers shouted, "Where you go missy?" or "Come sit down." There weren't too many that looked like they had enough passengers, so I just picked a reliable-looking silver taxi with only one other person. I loaded my large bag into the back and took a seat. I put my earbuds in to avoid the voices selling sardines, soft drinks, and cards to add minutes to your cell phone.

I sat there for a long time. No one else seemed to be getting in the taxi, despite the driver's efforts. I watched a green taxi going to my destination load three passengers. Time was ticking. Although I knew I could be fashionably late, I didn't want to verge on disrespect. I hadn't given the driver any money yet, so I grabbed my bag and went over to the green taxi. The driver tried to stop me. He wasn't happy that I was bailing on what he thought was a done deal. I apologized and said I had a meeting to go to, leaving him to complain to his sole passenger.

As I sat in the green taxi, which was even hotter due to the number of passengers, the silver taxi acquired six people—four in the back, two in the front—and they drove off. I cursed myself for being impatient. I was hot, tired, and ready for the trip to be over. And just like "Mama Liberia" often does, when you feel like you're at your breaking point, she does something that brings you back to her. Maybe it's a cool breeze, maybe it's someone who walks by selling exactly what you need at that moment, or maybe, on this day, you don't have to spend hours in a taxi station. "Mama" was there for me; our taxi left shortly after the silver one.

We were about halfway to the junction leading back to my village when we rounded a bend and saw it. Before my eyes understood what I was seeing, I heard someone say, "Oh God!" It must have happened just minutes before we arrived. People were running down the road, crying. The crowd grew by the minute. An SUV, looking undamaged, was pulled off to the left side of the road. A group of passengers stood outside of the vehicle, and a woman was crying. Then, off the road, past the ditch, in the bush, were the crumpled remains of the silver taxi. Limp, lifeless bodies were pulled out. I saw blood.

The driver, who had been so vexed with me earlier, was dragged partway toward the road before his rescuer ran back for others. The driver dropped to his knees, held his head, gushing with blood. It didn't seem real. But then he collapsed onto the steaming asphalt and didn't move again.

My green taxi had stopped and we all got out. The women I rode with yelled, "You were in that taxi! The white woman was in that taxi!" I stood quietly by our vehicle . . . and then the tears came. I felt ashamed. A truck drove up to load the bodies. Someone said they were taking them to the hospital in Kakata. Alive, motionless victims were loaded with the dead bodies. They lay in the hot sun for a half-hour as I stood in shock.

A somber man I didn't know came up to me and gestured toward our green taxi. He opened the door and motioned for me to get in, nodding his head as if to say it was okay to leave. On cue, with the other women passengers and me inside, the driver departed.

Our driver had taken cell phone photos to show locals in the next town to help identify the bodies. When we pulled up, people cried by the road, searching for the news of their loved ones. As our driver showed them pictures, people stared at me through the window, saying "the white woman is crying."

I wanted to yell. I wanted to scream. Yes! Of course, I am crying—just like these other women. But I remained silent, because I felt embarrassed for drawing attention to myself during such a horrible tragedy, ashamed that people were talking about me instead. The driver told the crowd that I had been in the silver taxi, and at the last minute, I had made my way into his.

Outside my car window stood a little boy with his friend watching me as tears rolled down my face. He said, "God saved her. God saved the white woman."

Victoria Zawitkowski was a Peace Corps volunteer in Sanoyea, Bong County, from 2016 to 2019. She taught high school math and English for two years, and then served as volunteer leader for one year. Victoria works as an education specialist for Planned Parenthood of the Rocky Mountains in Colorado. She likes to go hiking and camping with her Liberian dog, Kola.

A PEACE CORPS VOLUNTEER TRANSFORMED MY LIFE

BY SIAFFA T. KARNEH

One evening in 2013, I was in the resource room at Cuttington University. I always went there after my classes to spend time with a former Peace Corps volunteer named Rebekah Schulz and another student she was helping. I wanted to learn computers from Sis RB—when I started at Cuttington that semester, I did not even know how to turn one on—and prove I was as serious as the other student, who I considered my competition. But as usual, I felt sad. While the other student whom Sis RB had taught at Sanniquellie Central High School in Nimba County was applying for a scholarship that would pay for him to study in the United States, I did not see how I would find the money to stay at Cuttington. All I could think about was how I might need to leave and return to Monrovia, where people would mock me, saying I was not able to complete the work. They would not know I left the university for financial reasons.

Sis RB noticed my mood. "Why are you always sad? You're not happy."

"I'm worried," I said. "When the semester comes to an end, if I cannot pay my school fees, I will drop from school."

It was almost 5 p.m. when the generator cut off, and Sis RB closed the resource room. We were the last ones there, so we walked out together. As we began to cross the campus, she and I continued to talk.

"Make use of the opportunity you have and forget about the rest," she told me.

At that moment, I had hope. I knew that I would not be thrown out of school, even without a scholarship, if I worked harder. Before we reached the place where the path split, she left to go to her house while the other student and I went to our dorm. I was lively again.

After that, I stopped being anxious and was motivated to study harder to score high marks. I ended the semester with an encouraging grade report—a 3.5 GPA. When I showed it to Sis RB, she was excited and danced a proper African dance. From that day on, she paid for my entire tuition, food expenses, field trips, books, and even a stipend.

Sis RB supported me educationally and morally as well. I went to her for help on subjects I could not understand, especially math. In 2016, as usual, she sent the money for my tuition through Western Union, so I had it before coming on campus. Additionally, she suggested I try for a USAID/HELD scholarship, because getting it would look good on my academic record. I applied for it and received it.

All of this had not seemed possible when I was younger. I am a half-brother of nine siblings from my father's side and a half-brother of six siblings from my mother's side. My mom and dad broke up when she was pregnant with me. When my mother gave birth to me, she took care of me as a single parent until I turned fifteen. She dropped out of school because of the pregnancy and did not go back because the civil war erupted two years later, ending her educational sojourn. My father was also a high school dropout who was fortunate to work with the Peace Corps as a driver and expeditor. He worked diligently and won the admiration of almost all of his colleagues and the Peace Corps volunteers in Liberia, including Sis RB, who then taught high school math.

Sis RB was interested in helping serious but less fortunate students to accomplish their dreams by connecting them with foreign and local scholarship opportunities. She asked my father whether any of his children were interested in studying agriculture. My father told her I was. A scholarship became available at Earth University in Costa Rica the following year, so Sis RB gave the information to my father. Although my application was unsuccessful, Sis RB remembered me, even as her time as a volunteer ended and her new job with USAID began. She visited the Peace Corps office in Monrovia, saw my father, and asked whether I had started school. When he said no, she urged him to have me sit for the Cuttington University entrance exam. After I passed the test, Sis RB promised to pay for my credits for the first semester while my father covered the dormitory and food costs.

I wondered what would happen next. A single semester at Cuttington totaled one thousand one hundred and eighty dollars, which is a large sum of money in Liberia. Considering the number of children my father supported, he could not easily spend it on me alone. This worried me greatly as I started my studies. How could I ever afford eight semesters of college?

In 2017, thanks to Sis RB, I graduated with a B.Sc. degree in plant and soil science.

Today, I am a results measurement assistant for a program under the Adam Smith International NGO called GROW-Liberia. I work with cocoa farmers across Lofa County. I have not forgotten what Sis RB did for me. I am the only light on my mother's side—the only one who graduated from high school and college. I fully sponsor one of my half-siblings from my mother's side, who is still in elementary school, and partially sponsor another half-sibling attending the University of Liberia.

On the wall of Sis RB's house, she hung these words: "I'm in the world to change the world."

Seeing the number of people Sis RB helped, and how she went out of her way to sponsor someone she did not know, motivated me. You do not have to have much to help people.

Siaffa T. Karneh is a member of the Vai ethnic group. He is a 2017 graduate of Cuttington University in Suakoko, Bong County, where he earned a Bachelor of Science degree in plant and soil science. Since 2018, he has worked for an Adam Smith International program called GROW-Liberia.

PEACE CORPS MAN

BY JOHN W. MILLER

When I was young, the lights
of Broadway used to turn me on.
Africa changed that about me.
Liberia moved inside my head,
shouldering out the Great White Way.
Now I'd rather stroll the back streets of town,
of Coplay, Pennsylvania, my hometown,
of Pleebo, that other place I used to haunt,
but now it's Pleebo that haunts me.

Pleebo, that raucous crossroads
on Liberia's edge,
at the tip of West Africa's hump,
half another world away.
I loved the walk home
from school each day.
"How do-o, Peace Corps man?"
"How do-o?" kids would say.
"Hi!" I'd answer back,
just like in the USA,
But then I'd give them,
"Ah! I all-right-small!"
They'd laugh and run away.

Along the path, I'd see
old women bent above
cook pots simmering
on the fire.
"Come, let's eat!"
they'd call to me,
would share a sip
of soup and sympathy,
a handful of their rice.
"Yo' miss yo' home,
Peace Corps man?
We yo' home now,
so tell a story of America,
For the rice and soup.
Tell a story, Peace Corps man.
Tell a story!"

So I'd tell them all about Coplay.
About my pals, crazy dudes
like Fast Eddie,
Sammy B, Raymie, and the Doc.
About the Pennsylvania Dutch
and the odd way we have of talking
in the valley
where I first saw daylight.
"Yo' too funny, Peace Corps man!"
they'd say,
maybe understanding
only half of what I'd said.

"Oh! Wha' happeen?
Tell it all again!"
And so I would.

Most everyone is gone now.
All those I knew back then.
The war got them.
Or dysentery,

malaria,
cholera,
HIV/AIDS,
Ebola,
making farm,
childbirth,
life.

It was life, mostly.
It all catches up
with you there.
But, by God,
what a life!
Unless the madness
of power
and politicians
should invade and interfere.

It was life
out there on the edge.
On the edge
of Liberia.
On the edge
of time.

My life in Pleebo
was a peaceful
hole in time.
A gentle, lovely whole.

Here, it seems, the hole is full, mostly.
Filled with cell phones,
Facebook
fake news
Twitter
texting
sexting
fear

anger
hatred
emptiness . . .

An emptiness
we used to
fill with
life.

John Miller served as a Peace Corps volunteer in Liberia from 1981 to 1984 in Maryland County, where he taught English at Pleebo High School. John later served as assistant Peace Corps director for Peace Corps Ukraine from 1993 to 1996. He now teaches cross-cultural communication for the Air Force. His experiences as a PCV provide examples of effective—and ineffective—intercultural communication.

John with his Liberian students and friends, Pleebo 1981

GOODBYES ARE NOT FOREVER

BY STEPHANIE BACHMAN

My community worked so hard to get a Peace Corps volunteer. The school delayed other projects to convert their former kitchen into a house. It was a small, two-room building, but it was my home, and I was happy there. Living on the school grounds, I could not have asked for a shorter commute. Every morning, I did prep work on my porch for my general science classes. Since my school did not have a laboratory, I used whatever local materials I could find for demonstrations and low-resource labs with my students to convey the topics I taught.

One Wednesday morning in late November 2019, my cell phone dinged as I prepared for such a lab. Quickly, I saw a message telling volunteers to report to Kakata on Friday. I had class in fifteen minutes. I did not have time to ponder why we were meeting. I would deal with it after school when I could process it more.

After I finally read the message, it was not any clearer. Every volunteer received the same text about an all-volunteer conference on Friday. No information was given about the meeting except that it was mandatory. This led to much speculation amongst volunteers. As I scrolled through my phone, the group's consensus was that the meeting was related to the ongoing banking crisis. Most volunteers, especially those living far from Monrovia, such as myself, had been having trouble withdrawing money from the bank for weeks. Thoughts on what the Peace Corps staff would say varied. I was not sure how to feel or what to think.

The next day, I acted as if everything were normal. Internally, I knew it was not. I was in denial about what was coming, but I also had a feeling this could be my last time teaching my students. My seventh-graders had been acting out and causing trouble in class lately. I coped with these challenges by telling myself it was a problem for another day. Well, either that or something that I would never have to worry about again.

At the all-volunteer conference, we were informed that seventy percent of volunteers would be evacuated due to the ongoing economic crisis. This included me, since my site was slated for closure anyway, and I did not want to apply for one of the two dozen open sites. I had only recently moved to Baila due to unforeseen circumstances and a situation beyond my control. Knowing I would have to endure another relocation just three months after my last one kept me from applying to stay. Site changes are emotionally and mentally draining experiences, and it was not something I wanted to undergo again.

I lived in Baila, Bong County, about two hours north of Kakata on the main road. I delayed leaving Kakata on the Monday morning as much as possible, because I wanted to arrive after the school day ended. If feasible, I hoped to avoid seeing anyone until I delivered the news in the morning. Despite my best efforts, I returned as school let out. My students welcomed me back and proclaimed excitement for the next day's classes, while I pretended everything was all right despite the secret I carried inside.

The following day, I broke the news during a meeting with the school administration. So overcome with emotion, I could not sit down when my principal instructed me to do so. Nor could I find the words to explain the situation. Instead, I read the letter from the Peace Corps, but halfway through, I began to cry. When I finished, everyone but my principal left to start school. Alone, he hugged me, and our tears dripped onto each other's *lappa* attire. At that moment, I knew how loved and cared for I was after only a few months, especially since it was the only time that I saw a Liberian man cry.

"I thought you wanted to discuss the seventh-graders' behavior. I could not sleep last night," he said.

"Neither could I," I lamented.

First, my principal and I went to the ninth-grade classroom and broke the news. The entire class became visibly upset—stunned silence, jaws agape, and woeful sobbing. I had difficulty staying composed as I explained the situation. Next, I went to the seventh-grade classroom, and their reactions contrasted with the raw emotions and sadness of the ninth-graders. Conversely, they quietly sat still as if I had just announced I would be out of the classroom for two weeks instead of the remainder of the school year. After the brief pause, someone asked who their new teacher would be. Upset, my principal admonished them for seemingly caring about nothing else. In reality, the younger students processed the news differently. Later, I did an impromptu photo shoot with my students. It was a fun moment during an otherwise miserable day.

My going-away ceremony was incredible and emotional. Some students wrote and performed songs. One had the lyrics, "You came in September, October, and November, and now it is time for you to go." This highlighted how little I had been in Baila but how wondrous those few months had been. The farewell ceremony emphasized how different things were in Baila compared to my old site. It had taken three months and threats from my regional coordinator to get a welcome ceremony in my first community. I truly felt at home in Baila, and things were looking up in my service. Then, everything was taken away because of something beyond my control. The whole situation felt like a slap in the face.

In preparation for a Peace Corps volunteer, the school had spent a lot of time and money getting my house ready. When I arrived, the date in the concrete for the renovations was less than two weeks prior, and the whitewash had not even thoroughly dried. All that effort to get a volunteer, and I left after three short months, with no timeframe for when a new volunteer might arrive. Not only was I losing the place I called home, but my village was also losing a volunteer they had fought so hard to acquire.

Because of the abrupt nature of my departure, the goodbyes to my students, friends, and community felt rushed. I left without a true sense of closure. Returning to Liberia on my own was something I started contemplating within a few months of my evacuation. I figured a short visit would be doable before beginning a full-time job. However, COVID-19 delayed such plans because international travel was ill-advised.

Eighteen months after I left Liberia for what might have been the last time, I went back. This visit was brief, but it granted me the opportunity to spend quality time with my community. They welcomed me back with open arms as if no time had passed. I still had a home there. Now, I left with a proper farewell. My heart was full.

Because I never know what life may bring, I have learned to be grateful for all that I have in the moment. Goodbyes simply mean, "I'll miss you," until we meet again.

Stephanie Bachman served as a Peace Corps volunteer in Vaye Town, Gbarpolu County, and Baila, Bong County, from 2018 to 2019. She taught junior and senior high school students English, mathematics, physics, and general science. Now, she works as a physical scientist for the Environmental Protection Agency in Durham, North Carolina. During her free time, Stephanie enjoys cooking, reading, dancing, and spending time with friends and family.

Stephanie with her students on her final day, 2019

IT'S ALL IN A BOX

BY CATHY WARD

Actually, a plastic bin
with snap-lock handles
and a label taped on its end:
Peace Corps Liberia

I'm surprised it all fit,
two years of stuff
with memories folded into the
creases and spaces
between the pieces.
Wood, glass, bone, fabric,
Twisted into color, art, love, beauty.
Torn from a country fighting
for breath,
for peace.
Pressed into a suitcase and flown
far from familiar,
Compressed and repressed in a plastic bin.
Handles clicked shut
and pushed into a closet on the second story
where the stories inside
are muffled and struggling to breathe.

I click open an edge and lift the lid
A loud gasp comes from within
I whisper,
"Hello."
Piece by piece
I ease each memory up and out of the box
eager to see it unfold, stand, stretch, and remember.

This scratched-up green glass Club Beer bottle
will wait forever
to be returned, refilled, and redrained
down another happy throat.

A chunky wooden elephant,
tusks of bone,
a broken tail,
longing to return to its place
on the kitchen windowsill,
covered with thick smells of coal pot smoke
and simmering cassava greens.
Its big, smooth ears hold faint drumbeats,
the crunch of worn sandals on dusty pebbles
and the gentle flap of cotton drying on the line outside.

To my little neighbor friends,
Mondamah, Alice, and Fortee,
Who laughed and bounced
on the couch in my house:
I have your toys,
the three stoic monkeys
who will not see, hear, or speak evil,
carved from dark burgundy jungle wood.
Shiny from the oil in your small smudges.
Rough grooves have snagged fragments of your smiles,
and puffs of your breath.
The monkeys are magic, you told me
they keep you safe
from the soldiers
and the bullets.

My sundress made from bright red fabric
called to me at the market
then danced against my tanned, dusty legs
on those long walks to school.

Lone Star matches
stuck in a baggie
zipped closed.
Alone
without the sooty oil lamp
and drippy candles.
No clumsy fingers
slide open the tiny cardboard box
to find the hero
who will burst into the darkness
throwing happy shadows on the walls
glowing hope and warmth and safety.

Hours, days, and months woven into
colored squares
stitched into a blanket
by callused brown fingers,
sounds of children laughing
and dogs barking
shake out as I jiggle the wrinkles.

And now
They wait.
They know.
They prepare.
Once again,
slowly,
they are folded and tucked and snuggled
against each other,
with each other.
They hear the snap,
feel the lift,
hear the scratchy

slide onto the shelf.
Darkness breathes into the quiet.
I'm surprised it all fit.
In a box.

Cathy Ward and her husband, Charlie, had been married a year-and-a-half when they stepped off the plane in Liberia in January 1985. Their Peace Corps experience as education volunteers in Buchanan remains the most exciting and impactful adventure they have had in thirty-eight years of marriage. Cathy is a retired first-grade teacher and lives in Eugene, Oregon.

REFERENCE MATERIALS

LIBERIAN ETHNIC GROUPS

(MOST COMMON AND IN ALPHABETICAL ORDER)

1. Bandi
2. Bassa
3. Belle
4. Dey
5. Fula
6. Gbii
7. Gio
8. Gola
9. Grebo
10. Kissi
11. Kpelle
12. Krahn
13. Kru
14. Loma
15. Mandingo
16. Mano
17. Mende
18. Sapo
19. Settler (see Glossary)

LANGUAGE EXPRESSIONS USED IN THE BOOK

Gio greetings:	
Good morning	Ba bua
Response	Aa-oo
Kpelle greetings:	
Good morning	Ya wun
Hello	Ka tua (plural)
How are you/What news?	Ku Meni ju?
Bassa expression:	
Take time	Ma mu or Beta beta nu bek bek
Mende for "big sister"	Ngor
Loma for White person	Wii-kwelegi or Kwe
	Wii-kwe-legeius (plural)
Kpelle term for light-skinned foreigner	Kwi (see Glossary)
Loma for market table	Whee-la

GLOSSARY OF TERMS

Americo-Liberian – See "Settlers/Americo-Liberians."

Ancestor tree – A large tree in a village where the residents believe the spirits of their ancestors reside.

Bucket bath – To take a bath using a cup and a bucket of water.

Bush – The forest or jungle.

Bush meat – Any wild animal hunted and killed in the bush/forest to sell and/or eat for meat.

CARE – Cooperative for Assistance and Relief Everywhere is an international humanitarian organization fighting global poverty and world hunger by working alongside women and girls.

Chop – Liberian English for a prepared meal made of cooked rice topped with some form of soup (sauce) made from greens, vegetables, meats, or fish.

Coming to go – Liberian English for "about to leave."

Country cloth – Local hand-spun, hand-woven cotton cloth.

Dash – Bribe or a gift

Diazepam – The generic name for Valium, used for short-term treatment of acute repetitive seizures.

Diversity Visa Lottery – The Diversity Immigrant Visa program, also known as the "green card lottery," is a U.S. government lottery program for receiving a U.S. Permanent Resident Card. The Immigration Act of 1990 established the current and permanent Diversity Visa program.

Double words, such as "small, small" or "slow, slow" – a repeated word used to emphasize the meaning. Small, small = "very small."

Driver ants – Also known as Safari ants, driver ants are a large genus of army ants with powerful biting jaws that live in enormous colonies. Driver ants are found in tropical Africa.

Dry – Slim or skinny. Not used as a compliment, but out of concern that the person is not fat or healthy enough.

Dry rice – Plain, cooked rice

Expat – An expatriate, or expat, is an individual living and/or working in a country other than his or her country of citizenship, often temporarily and for work reasons. An expatriate can also be an individual who has relinquished citizenship in his or her home country to become a citizen of another.

Fufu – Liberian dough made from boiled and ground cassava root.

Ground pea/groundnuts – Peanuts. A major crop in Liberia used in soups or as snacks.

Hardship post – A name given by the U.S. Diplomatic Service to diplomatic posts in countries where living conditions are difficult due to climate, crime, health care, pollution, or other factors.

Headpan – A large, round, porcelain-covered tin pan used to carry market goods, crops, etc., usually carried on the heads of women while walking.

Heartman/heartmen – A term relating to the Liberians stories about men in the bush who work for medicine men to procure human organs for dark magic rituals.

Highlife music – A type of rhythmic, West African, popular music and dance that originated in Ghana in the late nineteenth century.

Houseboys/girls – Usually students who did housework, such as fetching and boiling water, general house cleaning, washing and ironing clothes, market shopping, and cooking. Houseboys/girls were paid a wage that provided a good income for young students to fund their schooling costs. Another option in exchange for these services was to provide the student with housing, meals, clothing, and school fees. These individuals were instrumental in helping foreigners to navigate cultural differences and to provide language translation.

In-country – Liberian term for "within the country."

Jollof rice – A rice dish served throughout West Africa, with onions, tomatoes, hot peppers, meat, or other vegetables.

Kittilee/kittley – A small, bitter vegetable related to an eggplant that is the size of a pea cooked into a sauce.

Kofte/kofta/kafta – Balls of ground meat often grilled on a stick, introduced to Liberia by the Lebanese.

Kol tar – Liberian English for "coal tar:" a Liberian term for a paved/asphalt road.

Kwi, kwe, or kwii – Various language spellings used throughout most of Liberia, meaning "light skinned foreigner."

Lappa – Two yards of African fabric that women wrap around their waists as a skirt. The term can also be used to refer to a complete outfit for a man or a woman made of this African fabric.

Liberian English – A pidgin version of American Black English of the 1800s, brought to Africa by the freed American slaves in 1820 and influenced by Liberian languages. It is the most widely used language in Liberia today.

Lone Star – Local brand of boxed matches named after the Liberian flag. Liberia is often called The Lone Star State.

Money-bus – A pickup truck with an open canopy used as public transport.

Monkey bridge – A traditional, handmade wood, bamboo, vine, or rope walkway built across a river or gully.

National exam – The national exam is an official exam given to all graduating seniors in Liberia. In the past, the exam was purely a Liberian-written and administered exam by the Government of Liberia. In recent years, Liberia joined the West African Examination Council (WAEC), a consortium of other English-speaking West African states, including The Gambia, Sierra Leone, Ghana, and Nigeria.

Palaver – A discussion, argument, or trouble (e.g., "money palaver," or "woman palaver"). Derived, probably indirectly, from Spanish or Portuguese. A palaver is not merely a discussion; it can be somewhat akin to a public debate.

Palaver hut – A round, open-sided hut consisting of wooden poles and a thatched roof where people gather to "palaver." It is similar to a public meeting hall.

Palm butter – A thick soup or sauce made from palm nuts.

Palm oil – A red oil extracted from palm nuts. The most common oil used for cooking in Liberia.

Palm wine – Sap is extracted from a live or fallen palm tree by a tapper. This white liquid sap is sweet and non-alcoholic, but after a few hours it ferments and becomes alcoholic in nature.

Pangolin/antbear – A scaly anteater.

Paramount chief – The English language designation for the highest-level political leader in a regional or local polity or country administered politically with a chief-based system.

PCV – Peace Corps volunteer

Pekin – Derived from "pickaninny," a Pidgin word used in Black American English in the 1820s, meaning "small black child."

Rice bag – A hand-woven bag made from the fibers of the raffia palm that people use either like a purse or to carry items or dry rice.

Ricebirds – A small brown bird that lives in large flocks in Liberia. These birds, known in other parts of the world as "Reed-birds, Rice buntings, or Bobolinks," congregate in the canopies of large trees with loud chattering in the mornings and evenings. They feed on fields of rice.

Road to Health Card (RTHC) – A folded, yellow card used to record the medical summary of a child's health in the first five years of life. The RTHC used in Liberia in the '70s recorded immunizations, weight, and general health.

RPCV – Returned Peace Corps volunteer

Runny belly – Liberian English for diarrhea

Schistosomiasis – An infectious disease, also known as "bilharzia," caused by parasitic flatworms that infect the urinary tract or intestines. The disease is spread by contact with fresh water contaminated with parasites released from infected freshwater snails. Symptoms include abdominal pain, diarrhea, bloody stool, or blood in the urine.

Settlers/Americo-Liberians – The name for the descendants of the freed American slaves who returned to the west coast of Africa in 1820 and declared the independent nation of Liberia in 1847. Americo-Liberian was a term used by Peace Corps volunteers common in the earlier decades. The term is less commonly used by Liberians today, and members of the "settler's group" definitely do not use it. The most common term is "Congo," which can be a mildly negative term. The most neutral term is "Settler," which is what academics and some government officials use.

Small goods – Small, dry goods, such as matches, batteries, candy, and gum.

Soup – What Liberians call "soup," most English speakers, including those from neighboring countries, call "sauce." Liberian "soups" include peanut sauce or palm butter, and are normally served over rice.

Sweet-o – Liberian English for "good' or "delicious."

Take time – A Liberian English expression meaning "slow down" or "take your time."

Upcountry – Liberian term for "into the interior of the country, away from the capital city."

USAID – United States Agency for International Development.

Words ending in "o" or "ya" – Many Liberian English words end with an "o" or "ya." It is the style of the language and does not change the meaning of the word. Example: "Thank you-ya.'

RESOURCES

Anthology goal: Our book of true Liberian stories and poems will safeguard our memories as well as promote Peace Corps' values by illustrating the Peace Corps' impact at home and abroad.

Friends of Liberia (FOL): http://fol.org/. Established by returned Peace Corps volunteers in 1985, the FOL is a non-governmental, non-profit organization seeking to positively affect Liberia and Liberians through education, social, health, economic, and humanitarian programs. The FOL now proudly includes Liberians, diplomats, missionaries, academics, development workers, and others committed to Liberia. The FOL's vision is to assist Liberia in its quest to be a peaceful and just country in which every Liberian has opportunities for quality education and employment and access to adequate health care.

Global Connection Program: https://www.peacecorps.gov/educators/global-connections/. Speakers are available to share more about our Liberia experiences with your school or organization, and can be requested on the Peace Corps website listed above. Click on the "Request a Connection" tab and complete the details about your school or organization. In the description section, note the name(s) of the Peace Corps volunteer(s), the story/poem in the book, and request Liberia as the Peace Corps country of service.

Peace Corps: https://www.peacecorps.gov and https://www.peacecorps.gov/liberia/. Established as a U.S. government agency in 1961, the Peace Corps provides a service opportunity for motivated American changemakers to immerse themselves in a community abroad, working side-by-side with local leaders to tackle the most pressing challenges of our generation. Since 1961, over two hundred and forty thousand Peace Corps volunteers have served in one hundred and forty-two countries around the world; over forty-three hundred volunteers have served in Liberia. The Peace Corps' mission is to promote world peace and friendship by fulfilling three goals: to help the people of interested countries in meeting their need for trained men and women; to help promote a better understanding of Americans on the part of the peoples served; and to help promote a better understanding of other peoples on the part of Americans.

National Peace Corps Association (NPCA): https://www.peacecorpsconnect.org
/cpages/home. The National Peace Corps Association is a 501(c)(3) nonprofit that is a mission-driven social impact organization encouraging and celebrating lifelong commitment to Peace Corps ideals. NPCA supports a united and vibrant Peace Corps community, including current and returned Peace Corps volunteers, current and former staff, host country nationals, family and friends, in its efforts to create a better world. By design, the Peace Corps and NPCA have a close and cordial relationship that fosters mutual respect and understanding. Yet, at appropriate times, the NPCA exercises its independence and challenges the Peace Corps, publicly and privately, to reform its policies and procedures. Friends of Liberia (FOL) is one of one hundred and eighty-two NPCA affiliate groups.

History of Liberia: For more detailed information, the three following recommended books contain broad historical information about Liberia:

- Pham, John-Peter. *Liberia: Portrait of a Failed State*, New York, 2004.
- Ciment, James. *Another America: The Story of Liberia and the Former Slaves Who Ruled It*, New York, 2013.
- C. Patrick Burrowes: *Between the Kola Forest and the Salty Sea: A History of the Liberian People Before 1800*. Bomi County Liberia, 2016.

Note: To learn more, visit https://www.worldcat.org/, which is the world's largest online library catalog. Once a zip code is entered, the reader will be directed to local libraries where the books in question can be found.

Other books published about Liberia can be found on the Friends of Liberia (FOL) website, http://fol.org/

DISCUSSION QUESTIONS

When reading our stories and poems, consider these questions for stimulating discussion and insight for a variety of group settings, such as book clubs, classrooms, community or government organizations, and faith-based communities.

1. If, as Neale Donald Walsch suggests, "Life begins at the end of your comfort zone," how do you think this was evident in the many of the stories of those who worked in Liberia?
2. Two Civil Wars, two coup d'états, Ebola, AIDS, and COVID-19 have taken a huge toll on the Liberian people. What clues do you find in these stories that help explain how and why they persevere?
3. Which three stories or poems depict ingenuity and resourcefulness at its best?
4. What value is there in living, working in, and experiencing another culture to the individual, to those around that person, and to the countries involved?
5. When some of the authors believed they had failed, what lessons did they learn?
6. Where did "White privilege" appear in these writings? How did it affect outcomes?
7. Who do you think learned more valuable life lessons, the Liberian people or the foreigners who worked there? Which stories/poems made you think that? Which stories best demonstrated the foreigners learning life lessons from Liberians?
8. Which story/poem surprised you the most? Why?
9. What can people from other countries learn from the Liberian people?

10. How would you feel if someone from a different country came to work in your community and brought ideas and teachings different from your own long held customs and beliefs?
11. In the story of your choice, explain how tolerance of different points of view benefited all involved.
12. Several stories speak of a long-lasting connection to Liberia and her people. What do you think drives that connection?
13. Which story/poem was your favorite? Why?
14. Which story/poem was your least favorite? Why?
15. Do you think you could work and live in another country at their salary and in their housing? Why or why not? What gifts might you bring? What gifts might you receive?

ACKNOWLEDGMENTS

As the African proverb states, "It takes a village to raise a child." In the literary world, it takes a large and fantastic team to publish a book. There are many FOL members and others to thank for their dedication, commitment, and volunteerism toward bringing our anthology to fruition.

FOL 2021 Board Members: Sarah Morrison, President; Rebecca Martinez, Vice President; Audrey Memmott, Treasurer; Karlin Scudder, Secretary; Kristen Grauer-Gray, Education Programs; Joseph (Joe) James, Economic Development Programs; Steve Pasinski, Small Grant Programs; Cori Maund, Health Programs; Victoria Zawitkowski, Communications; Maxwell Sines, Membership; Sally Zelonis, Development; Christine Sheckler, Member At-Large; Jo-Anne Manswell Butty, PhD, Member At-Large; Jefferson Krua, Member At-Large; and Richard (Ran) Nisbett, Member At-Large.

60th Anniversary Committee: Sarah Morrison, Don Drach, Linda Erickson, Dale Gilles, Jim Gray, Susan Greisen, Rebecca Martinez, Jim McGeorge, Audrey Memmott, Pat Reilly, and Stephanie Vickers.

Anthology Chief Editor: Susan E. Greisen

Submission/Reading Committee: Judy Marcouiller (Lead), Kelley McCready, Janet Riddle, Diane Trombetta, and Cathy Ward.

Editing Staff: Susan Corbett (Co-lead) Karen E. Lange (Co-lead), Stephanie Bachman, Jim Gray, Susan E. Greisen, John W. Miller, Pat Reilly, and Diane Trombetta.

Subcommittee/Task Force: Susan E. Greisen (Lead), Susan Corbett, Don Drach, Judy Marcouiller, Kelley McCready, and Rebekah Schulz.

Photographs: Owen Hartford, Garrett Mason, and all the FOL authors who submitted photos.

Anthology Intern: Joshua Dontae McFadden (Jan-April 2022, Stockton University, NJ)

Other contributors: Janie Mosely, Kally Reynolds and Robert Young, John Singler and Hamilton Hayes.

Publisher: Lisa Dailey of Sidekick Press, who collaborated with the FOL to publish this fine book.